Subconscious

Slap the face of fear and Wake up your subconscious

Robert K. Benson, MA, Ph.D. (cand.)

Dian Benson

To my friend Rhonda

Enjoy Buddy!

Be, Do, Have

Love always

May

July 10, 2004

© Copyright 2001 by Robert K. and Dian Benson. All rights reserved.

No part of this publication may be reproduced, stored in a retrieval system, or transmitted, in any form or by any means, electronic, mechanical, photocopying, recording, or otherwise, without the written prior permission of the author.

To contact the authors for presentations, workshops, personal SubContact Sessions or for any additional information:

Phone us at 1-250-707-1600
or Visit our Website:
www.subcontact.com
or
e-mail us: dian@subcontact.com

National Library of Canada Cataloguing in Publication Data

```
Benson, Robert K., 1936-
  Subcontact : slap the face of fear and wake up your subconscious
Includes bibliographical references.
ISBN 1-55369-012-5
  1. Self-actualization (Psychology)   I. Benson, Dian, 1946-
II. Title.
BF637.S4B46 2001              158.1            C2001-903303-6
```

TRAFFORD

This book was published *on-demand* in cooperation with Trafford Publishing.
On-demand publishing is a unique process and service of making a book available for retail sale to the public taking advantage of on-demand manufacturing and Internet marketing.
On-demand publishing includes promotions, retail sales, manufacturing, order fulfilment, accounting and collecting royalties on behalf of the author.

Suite 6E, 2333 Government St., Victoria, B.C. V8T 4P4, CANADA
Phone   250-383-6864   Toll-free   1-888-232-4444 (Canada & US)
Fax   250-383-6804   E-mail   sales@trafford.com
Web site   www.trafford.com   TRAFFORD PUBLISHING IS A DIVISION OF TRAFFORD HOLDINGS LTD.
Trafford Catalogue #01-0414   www.trafford.com/robots/01-0414.html

10   9   8   7   6   5   4   3   2

Dian's Dedication

To everyone who has the courage to ask questions of themselves and the willingness to go within to find the answers. You are the true freedom fighters of the world.

To my children, Sean, Kelly, Tim and Joe; may you find the courage and the will. And to my grandchildren, Indago, Zoë, Jax and Matt.

Bob's Dedication

To the next generation: to Carie, Carly and Cody; to Erin, Jarett and Jenna; to Jonathan, Kieran and Matthew; to Melina, Nicole and Shanna; and to Spencer and Tessa.

Dian's Acknowledgements

I am what I am today thanks to everything I have been.
Thanks to all my family and friends.
Thanks to Bob, the love of my life, without whom there would be no SubContact.
And to Em, thank you - we're just about there.

Bob's Acknowledgments

I am grateful that there was such a mind and spirit as Carl Gustav Jung. We found a mother lode in the tailings of his mind. Thanks also to my partner Dian, without whose tireless and scholarly enthusiasm there would be no SubContact.

Glossary of Terms

Change 101: a technique for examining and eliminating unidentified fears, especially the fear of change.

Conscious confusion: The use of cross sensory language to confound conscious awareness for the purpose of accessing the subconscious; e.g., hear the color, see the sound, taste the feeling.

Dolphinizing: the deliberate suspension of idea generation for a period of time to allow for subconscious material to be processed, which is followed by resumption of the ideation process. In a group context, dolphinizing is to stop spontaneous verbal ideation, allowing someone else to proceed.

Dream Language: a technique for examining dreams using four distinct elements to aid in understanding them. The elements are language, symbols, metaphors and context.

Ecological Change: change that is beneficial to every aspect of the organism: body, mind and spirit.

4th Dimension (4D) Thinking: a technique for new ways of thinking, solving problems and creating new ideas. Historically, there have been three ways of thinking. 4D Thinking describes the next step.

GO Teams: The power of mutual support groups is applied to a new concept in goal achievement.

Malaloopa: a term we coined to describe a 'bad loop', a circle of unwanted behavior that is repetitive. For example, to go on and off a diet with the promise of a food reward is a malaloopa.

Mental Imagery: the internal sensing of experiences that have no immediate outside source of stimulus.

PO: an abbreviation for Provocative Operation, a term coined by Edward de Bono (q.v.) for imposing a random word into a problem statement to create the movement of thought.

Power Meditation: a technique that emphasizes meditating for a specific purpose or goal.

Spiritual: we use this word to distinguish between organized religion, where God is interpreted for us, and the personal quest for God.

SubContact: a term we have coined to describe both a process and a technique. The SubContact *process* is a group of modular techniques, each complimentary to the overall goal of self-knowledge through contact with your subconscious mind. The SubContact *technique* is a guided meditation in which the subject is encouraged to verbalize a spontaneous story, which generally has a beginning, middle and an end. SubContact also refers to the overall *psychology* of conscious contact with the subconscious.

UF the Tragic Dragon: a personified symbol for Unidentified Fears.

> *"Come to the edge," he said.*
> *They said, "We are afraid."*
> *"Come to the edge," he said.*
> *They came. He pushed them*
> *… and they flew.* - G. Apollinaire

Contents and Index

Dedications and Acknowledgments	
Glossary	
Chapter 1	1
The Beginning	1
From the Journals of SubContact: Langley Store	1
Introduction	5
Examples of Change	6
About the Book	7
Bob's Story	10
Dian's Story	14
Chapter 2	17
Module 1 - Change 101	17
From the Journals of SubContact: Changing Hands	17
Change 101	20
The Nature of Change	20
Stages of Change - The 4 A's	21
Stage 1: Awareness	22
Stage 2: Acceptance	22
Stage 3: Action	22
Stage 4: Achievement	23
Time and the Movement of Change	23
Fear and Personal Change	24
From the Journals of SubContact: Natal Fear	25
The Nature of Fear	26
Looking for UF the Tragic Dragon	28
The Generation Gap	29
A Simple Guide to Knowing Fear	30
Four Steps to Identifying Fear	31
Step 1: Who?	31
Step 2: Why?	32
Step 3: How?	32
Step 4: What?	33
The Power of Understanding Our Fears	34
Concerning a Tragedy	35
From the Journals of SubContact: Overhead Burden	36
Chapter 3	39
Module 2: Power Meditation	39
From the Journals of SubContact: The Unseen Arch	39
Power Meditation	42
What is It?	42
The Benefits of Meditation	42
Getting Started	44
Fear Reviewed - UF the Tragic Dragon	44

How to Meditate	45
Sensory Mental Imagery	47
Communicating with our Subconscious	48
There is a Difference	49
Sample Guided Imagery	50
The Creative Tunnel	50
Chapter 4	**53**
Module 3: Dream Language	53
From the Journals of SubContact: Don Knotts	53
Dream Language	55
Understanding Dreams	56
Dream Element 1: Language	57
Dream Element 2: Symbols	58
Archetypes	59
Dream Element 3: Metaphors	61
Dream Element 4: Context	63
Day Remnants or Residue	64
What to do with Dream and SubContact Material	66
From the Journals of SubContact: The Cognoscenti	66
SubContact Analysis	71
Running Interpretation - Language	71
Symbols in the SubContact Session	74
Metaphor in the SubContact Session	76
Context of the SubContact Session	76
The Medium is the Message	77
Chapter 5	**79**
Module 4: 4th Dimension Thinking	79
From the Journals of SubContact: The Creativity Room	79
4th Dimension Thinking	82
1st Dimension Thinking (1D)	83
2nd Dimension Thinking (2D)	84
3rd Dimension Thinking (3D)	85
4th Dimension Thinking (4D)	86
Guidelines for 4D Thinking	86
Future Thinking Techniques	88
PO - Forward to this SubContact	89
From the Journals of SubContact: Break a Leg	90
Venturing Farther into 4D Thinking	93
The Collective Unconscious and the Internet	95
Brainstorming	96
The Creative Process and Practice	96
Creativity and Balance	97
PMI - Removing Emotion from Yes-No Decisions	97
Summary of 4th Dimension Thinking	99
Chapter 6	**100**

Module 5: SubContact	100
From the Journals of SubContact: The Cognoscenti Revisited	100
SubContact: Conscious Contact with our Subconscious	103
What Kind of Psychology is SubContact?	104
SubContact and C. G. Jung	105
SubContact and Sigmund Freud	107
SubContact and Cognitive-Behavioral Therapy	108
SubContact and Gestalt Therapy	108
SubContact and the 12 Step Program	109
So How Do We Do SubContact?	109
SubContact Guidelines	110
1. Preparation	110
2. Protocol	111
3. Procedure	113
4. Post-SubContact	116
Note for the Guide	118
A Sample Meditation Script for a SubContact Session	119
Going it Alone	120
Chapter 7	122
Module 6: GO Teams	122
From the Journals of SubContact: Growing Water	122
GO Teams	126
A Brief History	126
The Dynamics of Mutual Support Groups - MSG	128
Why the Name GO Teams?	129
Checklist for Forming GO Teams	130
Join a GO Teams Online	131
SubContact of Others	131
From a SubContact Session of 'S'	132
Chapter 8	137
The End of the Beginning	137
From the Journals of SubContact: The Revolutionist	137
Something Happened	139
What SubContact has done for us	141
Research Conclusions	142
Conclusion 1: Generalizability	142
Conclusion 2: Physical Balance	143
Conclusion 3: Mental Balance	146
Conclusion 4: Spiritual Quest	148
Nothing New Under the Sun	148
Quotations by Subject	149
Afternote	153
Bibliography	154

Chapter 1

The Beginning

This book includes two perspectives, one from within and one from without. As the authors, we provide the outer point of view. The inner perspective is reflected in the actual stories taken from the *Journals of SubContact*. Each chapter opens with such a story.

From the Journals of SubContact: Langley Store

I am in front of my neighborhood store as it was more than 50 years ago. Nothing has changed from when I was a little boy. The dark green paint on the wood framed door is flaking from the afternoon sun. The glass panels on the door have signs. One says "Drink Kik Cola" the other says "chew Wrigley's Spearmint gum". The thumb groove in the door handle is slightly misaligned so that a normal squeeze does not open it. I remember to apply a slight pressure to the right and the door swings open.

The dark hardwood floors are grooved with wear. A line of light bulbs hangs on plain electric wire from the ceiling. There is a magazine rack on the left and I can see Life, Redbook and Saturday Evening Post. To the right at the counter is old Mr. Langley, wearing his usual white apron as he serves a matronly customer.

They seem unaware of my presence and as much as I'd like to say something to the old gentleman, I am drawn to the back of the store. A dark flannel curtain separates the storefront from Langley's living quarters. I pull the blanket to one side and step into Mr. Langley's private living area. The entire space is about 12 feet by 12 feet and includes a small sink, hotplate, cupboard, a pan and a kettle. There is a small toilet cubicle behind a blanket curtain.

The rest of the back of the store is devoted to stock. I walk along a narrow corridor and notice a case of con-

densed milk, assorted cans of Campbell's soups, a carton of Dad's cookies and other assorted goods in assorted quantities.

I turn right and see a blue door bathed in liquid white light. It is a pure shade of dark blue, yet as I approach the door I see that it has the hint of some other shades of many different blues that come from many repaintings over the ages. There are scrapes and scratches that reveal an underlying black patina. I put my hand on the shiny dented doorknob and, after a moment, turn it. The door opens inward and as I step across the threshold I am aware of passing under the shadow of the doorway and experience a thrill of fear.

I am in a blue room with indirect lighting coming from every surface. It's like the set of a Stanley Kubrick movie. A man is waiting there for me. He has a regal presence although he holds a clipboard in the crook of his arm. He looks quite fit, tanned, about 55 and well groomed. He says to me, "I am Digital Man."

He does not have to explain what or who a 'Digital Man' is. For some reason I trust him completely and there is rapport between us.

"You are here to learn new things and my immediate task is to tell you that you have one chance in 10," he says.

I say to him, "That doesn't sound like very good odds."

He replies, "You must be very careful about the language here. Listen with your eyes and other senses as well as your ears. I did not say 'You have one chance in 10', what I said was 'You have an opportunity in digital matters'."

As soon as he says this I realize that I mistook his words 'an opportunity' to mean 'one chance' and had misinterpreted the digital symbols IO, I for on and O for off, as the number 10. But what is more important is that through misinterpreting I had changed his positive message into a negative one. He has demonstrated to me in an eloquent way to be careful of what I understand him to say.

The Beginning

The Digital Man leads me to another door and says, There is someone else for you to meet". As we leave that room and walk down a hallway I notice we cast no shadows and as I look around to understand why this would be I cannot detect a light source; the light seems to be distributed equally everywhere.

He opens the door and waits from me to pass through. A middle-aged man immaculately dressed in a dark suit with matching tie and pouf, waits for me at a small boardroom table.

My guide is walking slightly behind me and to my right and he says, "This is your Protocol Man." The new man studies my face as if he knows me but has never seen me before and is curious.

We shake hands.

He says, "We shall meet from time to time. There are rules to follow here. The number one rule is that you must believe everything you see, hear and feel when you are here. No matter how illogical it may seem, you must believe it is actually happening, because it is.

The second rule is do not edit your words before you speak them. If you do this you will defeat your purpose in being here. Anyway, you will be corrected.

Next is to trust your intuition. Report your instinctive feelings as well as what you actually see, hear and feel.

Next, never come in here unless you feel calm and positive. Always leave your fears, worries and anger at the door. If you cannot let go of your negative feelings, postpone your visit for another time.

Number five is that you will always find at least two meanings to any message you receive here. When you receive an answer to a specific question that is important to you, look past the first answer and you will find more understanding of the answer as well as the question. Additional meanings enrich and confirm your original understanding.

Next, the medium is the message. It will take you some time to understand this aspect, but understanding will come.

When you do comprehend, you will be ready to teach and write about it.

And finally, although you may come to believe that you can predict the future based on your experience here, remember that the future is unknowable. This is so because mankind has free will and free will and predictability are incompatible. The best you can expect to foresee is probability."

I know he is finished and I stand up along with my guide. Protocol Man shakes my hand and says, "You may come back to ask questions any time." I notice he hangs on to my hand and in an endearing gesture, much as old Mr. Langley used to do when I was a boyhood customer, Protocol Man puts his other hand over mine for a moment.

My guide leads me out and along a corridor still bathed in blue indirect light. As we walk he says, "Even though I'm the one devoted to the absolute science of digits, on-off, yes-no, black-white, I emphasize the importance of believing everything you see, hear and feel. There will be times when you experience the implausible, the unlikely, the illogical. You must believe it to be true."

He pauses at a door and says, "And now I am to show you something you shall always remember"

We step into a very large room, a room notable for the blue wall on the far side that curves toward us as if it is part of an enormous circle. We walk toward the wall. My guide stops and turns sideways to me, glancing momentarily at the clipboard he still holds. He reaches for a button on the wall and the entire height of the center of the wall begins to slide apart sideways. My perceptions reel from what I see and, as I begin to take in what is behind that wall, I realize that my concept of energy will never be the same again.

My first sense is that unimaginable power is inside the arc of that wall. I am awed. Words fail me. I cannot make sense of what I see. I begin to comprehend what it's like to understand both sides of a paradox in the same moment. Two rivers of pure energy rush in opposite directions simultaneously within the same vertical space. I have no illusions that such energy could be contained within that wall, and therefore know that it continues elsewhere in this universe. The dominant color is green although both streams vary from near white to yellow to dark green in unpredictable waves. I know intuitively that the velocity of each river is the speed of light.

There is a sound that is as exotic as it is harmonious. It is like a fluid resonance combining hiss and tone that is what music would look like if we could see it in motion.

I am afraid to approach the awesome power although I notice my guide is quite comfortable as waves of reflected light wash over him. He stands close to the open door and I wonder what would happen if he got caught up in the slipstream - surely he'd be torn two ways in the countercurrent. As if to answer my question he places his hand inside the river of energy. Nothing happens; even the sound does not change.

Digital Man slowly withdraws his hand and in the same motion pushes the button and the door begins to slide over the river of energy. He turns to me.

"You are tired and it's time for you to leave here now. You will come to call this place SubContact. In time, all that you've seen and recorded here will make sense to you. For now, my friend, good night."

The SubContact ends.

Introduction

Langley Store was the first guided meditation session that we came to call SubContact. It occurred at Calgary, Alberta, Canada in April of 1991. Guided meditative sessions preceded this one, but this was the definitive and seminal session that named the process, specified procedures, suggested The Journals of SubContact and foreshadowed seminars and the writing of this book.

The process of SubContact was born from the relationship of its authors, Bob and Dian Benson. Working together in a labor of love, we discovered that exciting results could be obtained by the systematic exploration of the subconscious. It was as if we discovered a symbolic door, opened it and passed beneath its arch to begin an adventure. It changed our lives.

What happened after we entered that archway and what our discoveries can mean to you is the subject of this book. From the beginning, we have set out to provide a simple guide, written in everyday language, to help you create and manage change in your life. SubContact explains techniques to access and understand your subconscious for the purpose of making personal changes. These techniques have evolved as a result of our thorough investigation and practice. Working together as co-explorers and co-authors, our experiences with SubContact helped us create positive, often dramatic changes in our own lives. With effort, you too can achieve personal goals and come to a greater understanding of the person you were always meant to be by following the path we describe in these pages.

Examples of Changes

What are some examples of the changes we've experienced? Individually and together we've: overcome addictions, conquered recurring bouts of depression, trained for and run marathons, earned university degrees, created and executed marketing concepts, conducted seminars and workshops, come to terms with our past, studied and taught in foreign countries and improved our health. For the first time, each of us enjoys a lasting relationship built on genuine partnership. We have swept from our lives unreasoned fears that once daunted us. We've experienced a lot of positive change in our lives since that first time we walked through an imaginary archway to begin SubContact. Today we lead rich and satisfying lives.

About the Book

SubContact is the term we have created to describe contact with the subconscious mind. Thus the many different kinds of experience we can have with our subconscious, such as dreaming, intuition, mental imagery or meditation, are all forms of SubContact. When SubContact is used to describe the technique we have developed, it refers to a specific type of guided interactive mental imagery. An additional meaning of SubContact is the program of modules we have developed to help others achieve a meaningful relationship with their subconscious.

The modules are presented in the order that SubContact evolved. The reader may choose to experience the modules differently. Each of the modules is self-contained and designed to be adaptable to personal needs. Each module overlaps and relates to the other modules.

The first module, Change 101, deals with the nature of, need for, obstacles to, and techniques for facilitating change. We all want change, we all fear change and we all experience change. We can choose to be an active partner to change, or we can allow ourselves to be buffeted by the fear of change. Using a simple formula for understanding fear, we show how to understand common damaging behaviors and the reason why our fears are obstacles to lasting change. The lessons in Change 101 can be used as a life-long practice to keep us in emotional balance and help us to understand why we fear change. Finally, for those fears that are reluctant to identify themselves, we demonstrate how we can turn to our inner selves for the answers. There we will begin to explore the wealth of wisdom available from our subconscious memories.

The key to unlocking our personal files of belief systems, and how it affects our reaction to change, is found in the second module, Power Meditate. Here we cover the techniques and psychology of contact with the subconscious, a preliminary to the practice of SubContact. We do not join the debating psychologists who are 'for' or 'against' the existence of the subconscious. Our book is about experience. It is about how we changed as the result of our relationship with our subconscious, and how our readers, if they choose, can make changes by exploring their own subconscious.

One of the discoveries we made was in the area of language. Understanding the information retrieved from the subconscious challenged us to interpret it. We have never spoken to anyone who, when their dream was analyzed from a purely linguistic point of view, was not amazed at the message it contained. Our subconscious, everyone's subconscious, is a master wordsmith, symbol maker and storyteller. Dream Language is a module that shows us how we can learn to recognize our own personal SubContact language. It draws on our experiences that have accumulated over a lifetime and, therefore, has meaning specifically within the context of our lives. Through practice at decoding our subconscious language, we can better understand the dialogue that takes place between our inner and outer worlds. Who doesn't wonder about the meaning of life and our place in the grand scheme of things? Perhaps our subconscious has offered us answers, answers that we could not understand. We suggest that the elements of Dream Language offer a way to make sense of the answers.

In 4TH Dimension or 4D Thinking we demonstrate that posing the question can be half the answer. Thinking in the 4th dimension is a method of using the subconscious mind to generate ideas and solutions. Although it is often said that two heads are better than one, the greatest benefit to learning and practicing this technique is in finding answers that fit us personally. The steps are straightforward and like anything we learn, the more we practice, the better we get at it and the easier it becomes.

Now we are prepared for the SubContact module that tells us everything we need to know to directly experience the wonder of conscious contact with our subconscious. When we take the time to understand our fears, then learn to set aside our conscious awareness, we can pass through that imaginary archway to our subconscious.

It is an archway that we, as co-explorers, have passed through many times as we researched SubContact. Now, acting as guides to point the way, we outline the protocols that worked for us. We also know that each person that continues to practice SubContact will be guided by her or his own unique process.

And finally, one way to practice all the techniques found in the SubContact modules is to be part of a goal-oriented group we call GO Teams. This final module of our program is a mutual support environment that provides us with an opportunity to establish goals and work toward them. Our experience shows that a particularly useful way to practice SubContact is to have a purpose or a goal to achieve. With a GO Teams approach, we have the additional benefit of like-minded individuals to help us get going, keep going, and get there.

As co-authors we worked as a team, supporting each other to develop what we uncovered. Together we learned to adapt it to our lives and to share it with others. Remember, it only takes two to make a GO Team.

All the modules of SubContact are designed to assist in accessing and understanding our subconscious experience, an experience that can enhance our well being, help us achieve our goals and live a more satisfying and fulfilling life.

We begin by telling our stories; what brought each of us to that point of awareness and acceptance of the need for change in our lives. We then describe how we began the exploration of our subconscious through guided meditation. When we realized the potential wealth of information available to us, we began to study and take notes on the language of the subconscious. We recorded our SubContact sessions. We experimented with creative problem solving, which lead us to 4th dimension thinking. We shared our work with others and the concept of support teams evolved for achieving goals.

We, Dian and Bob, began the process of making major life changes out of necessity. As a result of the successes we've had through the practice of SubContact, we continue to address the challenge of change for the satisfaction and meaning it brings to our lives.

Whether you think you know exactly what you want or are searching for that missing something, we guarantee that you will experience your life in a deeper, more satisfying way by doing what we have learned to do.

If you want it to, this book can change your life.

Bob's Story

I decided I would die on October 31, 1988. Mired in self-pity, blind to anything but my own sense of failure, I was corporately, personally, and spiritually bankrupt - and alcoholic. I decided the misery must end.

For a man with less than high school education I had been relatively successful. My employment history had been notable for a pattern of rapid rises to senior management positions. In my forties, I had created my own enterprise, and for several years I owned and operated an innovative and successful business. But though apparently riding a rocket of achievement, I was on a collision course with a humiliating and depressing defeat, a downfall assured by the fact that my business decisions were impaired by frequent drinking bouts.

I was 52 years old when my business crashed and ill prepared for the failure, the accompanying shame and subsequent age discrimination that barred me from meaningful employment. Heck, I thought companies would be glad to get hold of a person with my experience. When that belief proved illusory, my deflation was complete.

I selected two weapons to accomplish my goal of self-destruction: 76 Halcion tablets combined with a 40-oz. cocktail of Smirnoff vodka (to leave me, literally, breathless). I had closely followed news reports of a prostitute who had been convicted of the manslaughter of her john by slipping him one or two Halcion tablets and some booze. I reasoned that if one or two tablets with some drinks could kill a person, then a bottle of each would accomplish the deed with certainty.

Whereas the client's demise was unplanned, mine was deliberately timed. I owned a million-dollar insurance policy, which had been in force for a sufficient number of years that it would pay off in the event of suicide. Such were the original premiums that the equity accumulated in the policy would keep it in force without further contributions, until November 1st. Thus on a day set aside for trick-or-treating, having learned a trick or two from news reports of the hooker's testimony, I checked into a 5 star hotel, placed the "Do Not Disturb" sign on the door, and treated myself to the witch's brew.

Somehow I survived that murderous cocktail and awoke 24 hours later to behold a weak autumn sun through my hotel window. I was befogged. I became aware that my sense of future time no longer existed. I had no idea what I was going to do in five minutes, let alone five hours. A future period involving five days was impossible for me to envision. Having intended to eliminate my future, I had not anticipated the possibility of having to deal with it. It was like having a wall of fog in front of me, and the present and the past were the only reference points I had. This phenomenon predominated for at least two weeks, when gradually a sense of future began to re-establish itself.

I have never heard of this psychological phenomenon where one's sense of future is lost, although I am quite sure other people who have attempted suicide, and had every reason to believe they were going to die, have experienced it. In a great irony, I had dwelt so much on a failed past that I had planned to eliminate my future. As a consequence of my unexpected survival, I had to relearn to think in terms of what was yet to come.

It was necessary for me to come to terms with the astonishing fact that I had survived in spite of the massive doses of chemicals I had consumed. At first I sought a scientific explanation. The bed I had awakened in was somewhat rumpled, but free of vomit. If I had thrown up the chemicals that would have explained my continued existence. Likewise, the bathroom was in pristine condition, so it is unlikely that I had staggered in there during a blackout to eject the contents of my stomach. The toilet was still wrapped in a banner proclaiming that it had been "Sanitized For Your Protection". The shower was dry. The double-glazed windows of the hotel room were incapable of being opened.

I concluded, as many survivors do in such inexplicable circumstances, that it just wasn't my time. Which of course implies that there is such a thing as 'my time'. Coming to grips with this concept left me with little alternative than to entertain the possibility of the existence of 'God', whoever or whatever that might be. If my language betrays some reluctance on this matter, it's only because I had dismissed such a concept for the previous 12 years. I had attended AA meetings whenever my drinking created a crisis in my life, which was fairly frequently, but I had never put more than three continuous months together without picking up another drink. The part of the program that turned me off the most was AA's insistence, framed palatably as a 'suggestion', that there was a 'Power greater than myself', namely God.

As the saying goes, that was then – this is now. Today my life is a series of adventures, full of richness and joy beyond the imagining of the depressed, suicidal washout that I was. My part of this book is dedicated to sharing with you what I have learned about dealing with adversity, and what I now do when I face such obstacles.

I had allowed my previous existence to go spiritually, mentally and physically unchallenged. As the result of my unexpected survival, it was necessary for me to address each of these life domains.

I developed a philosophy of life less centered on myself, and one that acknowledged the existence of God. It was not possible to accommodate this change of view without also being more charitable in my regard for my fellow creatures, whether person or animal. A day does not pass without some form of communication between myself and the God of my understanding. As part of my spiritual awakening, I have come to conclude that there is a direct and positive relationship between a spiritual belief and empathy for others.

My previous obsession with alcohol had also dulled my mind. Such mental activities as curiosity about the world around me went unfulfilled. About four years after my recovery, at the age of 58, I enrolled in college. I crammed to make up for my lack of high school credentials, and achieved an Associate of Arts degree in 1995. At the end of the following year I obtained a Bachelors Degree magna cum laude in Psychology from the University of the State of New York. Two years later I successfully defended my Masters thesis.

I was accepted by the University of Queensland in Brisbane, Australia, to continue the pursuit of my formal education. At the end of the first year I received confirmation of my Ph.D. candidacy. My research is focused on the process of change. I recite these dates and milestones as a matter of record, and to strongly suggest that I successfully regained the use of my mental faculties, which had lain fallow for so long. Today I am a qualified psychologist.

My physical condition was also in need of an overhaul, and I went about changing this aspect of my life as well. During my entire adulthood I had never engaged in anything more vigorous than a round of golf, which was almost inevitably followed by several rounds of drinks.

Now things had to change; I had to get a grip on my physical condition. At first I walked, and then I walked faster, and then I walked and jogged until eventually I jogged marathon. I completed my first marathon when I was 57, another when I was 60, and I completed the Australian Gold Coast Half Marathon at the age of 63. Training for and running a marathon distance provided me with a capacity to endure, so it is not surprising that my physical rehabilitation immediately preceded my educational endeavors.

This book describes how I went about the task of creating massive changes in my life with the help of SubContact. Change is scary, and I went through a period of fear. But day by day, making use of my newfound self-understanding, I managed a transformation in my way of living. A large part of this book is devoted to how anyone can come to grips with personal change, and the fear that is its companion.

My education in Psychology and my life experiences prepares me to bring to you the latest developments in our research. In this book you will find a bias toward what is called 'Positive Social Science', which focuses on why things go right, rather than why they go wrong. This approach addresses imbalances in the history of psychology to date when, during the past three decades for example, 46,000 papers were written on depression, but only 400 studied joy.

It is a joy for me to join my partner Dian in attempting to bring some joy to your life, and to bring the wisdom of the ages, as interpreted through our experiences, to you.

Welcome to SubContact.

Dian's Story

Standing in my kitchen that New Year's Day, talking to a sick, very hung-over woman I had never met before, I saw for the first time a reflection of myself as I might become. All I had to do was pick up another drink and it would only be a matter of time. It was not what I wanted for my life.

For the past year or so I had been going to a twelve-step support group for family and friends of alcoholics. I knew very little about alcoholism before I attended that first meeting. I did know that my then husband fit a stereotypical profile depicted in a television special about the affects of drinking. At the end of the show the station listed the local phone number for the self-help group. One year later I called that number and went to my first meeting. That simple action began a process that would continue to bring positive changes to my life.

I learned about alcoholism, how it affected the alcoholic and the other family members. I came to think of my former husband as having an illness over which he had little or no control once he started drinking. But still I was afraid because of the violent behavior that was a part of his drinking. I lived in constant fear of the alcoholic, afraid to stay and afraid to leave. Eventually, realizing that I had my own choices to make, I faced my fear, took my three small children and left.

Without the practicing alcoholic to focus on, I began to look at the steps of the program for myself, especially the step devoted to taking a personal inventory. I admitted that many of the difficult and unpleasant situations from my past involved my drinking. Even though I stopped drinking when I became pregnant with my first child, I had had my share of drinking, getting drunk, having blackouts, and doing some crazy things. Yet, I did not deliberately set out to get drunk every time I took that drink. I learned that these were the symptoms of chronic alcoholism, an illness of the body, mind and spirit. From there, it was a simple deduction to make the diagnosis. I was an alcoholic. But it wasn't until that New Year's morning that I felt okay with it. I saw with clarity, for the first time, that I could never guarantee that one drink would be my only drink. I also knew that I wanted to live the rest of my life as a sober person.

With that realization I said to the young woman in my kitchen, "I'm an alcoholic, and there is a better way." When I said those words, I felt as if something ran up my back and left me. From that moment, twenty-five years ago, to the present writing of this book, I have enjoyed the feeling of that freedom. I believe, through Grace, that I had been relieved of the desire to ever take another drink of alcohol. I also felt that I needed to do a few simple things to safeguard my freedom. I joined a support group for alcoholics; I continued the process of examining my fears, and I did what I could to be of service to others. Living life on life's terms became a lot easier; yet I still experienced unexpected bouts of depression.

I never did tell my doctor about 'feeling the blues'. I was sure that any doctor's solution for me would be the use of mood-altering drugs. I had heard other women speak of their addiction to prescription drugs and how they needed to stop using any kind of mood altering drugs to live a 'sober' life. I was afraid I too would be addictive to these drugs, and intuitively, I was probably right.

When I recognized I was depressed, I learned there were some things I could do to help myself. I went to meetings. I talked. I listened to others, or as 'luck' would have it, I would get a call for help from someone feeling worse than I was. These actions often helped me to take a different perspective where I was able to count my blessings and get on with my life. But not always. There were times when an unshakeable despair threatened to overcome me, and I wondered what was wrong with me. It wasn't until Bob and I met and began to access our subconscious through guided imagery that I was able to find any answers.

Within a year of practicing SubContact, I was set free from that constant malaloopa of depression. The answers lay buried deep in my childhood memories. Fears had been suppressed that I was unable to reach until we began to explore and learn the language of the subconscious. Understanding the origins of these fears helped me move towards a self-confidence that I never had before. Together with this new awareness, the support of my partner and a little faith in a power that I choose to call God, I faced new challenges and achieved goals I could once have only imagined.

Today, my partner and I continue to live rich, fulfilling lives. It is our hope, as we share our experiences of SubContact within these pages that you too will feel encouraged to know yourself better. We invite you, here and now, to let your adventure of SubContact begin.

Chapter 2

Module 1: Change 101

From the Journals of SubContact: Changing Hands

It looks like dawn and I'm walking along a narrow, cobblestone street with a middle-aged man. It looks like an old English setting, probably London, and obviously a long time ago, maybe mid-1800s. Once in a while I catch a glimpse of a river, probably the Thames. The man is talking to me as we walk. He has a determined stride.

"Nothin' changes in my life. I get so weary of the same thing day after day. Get up 'fore the rooster, don't disturb Martha. Get to the factory on time or get jobbed. Work all day with that steam machine that hates me," he says, waving a bandaged left hand. "Go home after dark. Day after day's the same. I long for change," he says.

"Careful what you wish for sir, you might get it. What happened to your hand?" I ask, pointing to the soiled bandage.

"The Stamper tried to git it, but just caught a wee bit," he replied, holding it up and giving a cursory examination to the yellow spots in the center of the bloodstains on the grimy dressing.

"A machine tried to hurt you? I've never heard of such a thing."

"That's 'cause ye've never worked with one of them steamers. They're as ornery as they are strong. Gotta stay alert mornin', noon and night or somethin'll happen. Anyway, I'd just like some change in my life, any change from what I'm livin' now."

"Why don't you start by changing the bandage?"

He maintains his stride as he turns to me and says in a chiding way, "Don't go getting smarmy on me. I don't abide it more'n the next man. I kin take what's dished out. I don't want much, just some change from time to time."

I notice the inconsistency of what he said and in spite of his testy nature I say, "You want to change but you also want to be like the 'next man'. Sounds inconsistent, sir."

"Change's as good as a rest, they tell me."

"Why don't you find a different job, one without machines?"

"I ain't got time to look."

"What about moving to the country? Life is simpler there."

He looks at me quizzically and says, "Everyone's movin' to the city to get jobs in the factories, and you want me to move to the countryside? Ye're daft."

"Can't abide that any more than the next man, right?"

"Fer God's sake, Lad, some things'll never change, it's supposed to be this way. Anyway, here's where I work and ye'd best hie if ye want to stay with me."

He turns and walks under an archway made of brick. Inside is a huge, dimly lit factory. I can hear the roar of controlled fire and the hiss of impatient steam. I cannot see all the way up through the rafters, but I know the frame building is high because I can see wide pulleys and belts disappear into the gloom. The array of machinery is awe-inspiring: there are flywheels taller than a man and crane-like structures twice as high as the flywheels. The leather belt that connects the pulleys twists into a languorous figure eight, twenty feet along and fifteen feet above the packed earthen floor.

"Steams up, Will," a voice calls out, "Best get stampin'"

I look to see the source of the voice and see the shadow of a large man laboring in front of a furnace a hundred feet away.

My companion grunts, "That's Mal," and walks over to a lever that stands about four feet out of the ground. He grips the handle and with tremendous effort ratchets it back. Almost immediately a shriek of protest comes out of the ceiling as pulleys begin to turn for another day. The leather belts groan in sympathy and then start to flay about as if seeking vengeance.

My companion, Will, steps forward to a high table. There is a hole in the center of it and he stares at it as if reading its intent. He keeps staring at the hole even as he reaches over for another lever. Finally he breaks the stare and releases the lever, moving back a few inches as he does so.

Far above, I distinctly hear a snick *and then a* clack *and then a huge piston slams down into the hole,* WHAM, *pauses, then jerks up and out of sight again. Waiting, as if to catch the rhythm of the colossal machine, Will observes the timing of two more cycles, then turns and lifts a stack of thin circles of metal onto the table beside him. He waits for the* snick, clack, WHAM *and then, like the conductor of a discordant orchestra, he slips a sheet of tin-like metal over the hole and up against a template set in the table. For a breath of time Will's hand and wrist cover the hole as he snugs the metal up to the template, then he pulls back.* Snick ... clack .... WHAM *and the hammer from hell smashes into the metal sheet and withdraws. Quickly, yet fumbling slightly with his injured hand, Will twists the edge of the sheet that protrudes from the hole and withdraws what looks like a tin basin. This, then, must be his product, a pan used for washing hands. Quickly Will sets the basin on a wooden platform built slightly above the packed ground, then turns back to grasp another sheet and place it in position just before the* snick *and* clack *heralds a fresh onslaught:* WHAM!

Only a few moments of actual time go by, but it is as if I've been there beside Will and his monstrous machine all day. The cycle is repeated endlessly - snick *then* clack *then* WHAM, *although I notice that the first sound, the slightest one, becomes weaker as the day goes by.*

Then something happens. Will had been talking to me, forming short staccato sentences of displeasure about his unchanging life. He never tore his eyes away from the hole in the table but spoke to me through the side of his mouth, "Nothin' changes, never will" he said.

As he was placing a new sheet up against the template, high above something went awry with the sequence and there was no snick, only the clack. Will blinked, there was time enough for that, but not nearly time enough to pull his hand away. I could see recognition in his eyes, the immediate and absolute knowledge that his life will never be the same again.

The SubContact ends.

> *"It's not so much that we're afraid of change or so in love with the old ways, but it's that place in between that we fear..."* - Marilyn Ferguson

Change 101

Although any discussion based on our experience of personal change must include its inseparable companion fear, we begin by exploring the nature of change. Our focus is personal change and the four stages that we identify as necessary for successfully creating and managing it. Later in this chapter we will discuss the parasitic nature of hidden fears. But first, let's examine change itself.

The Nature of Change

There are three kinds of personal change: natural change that comes with time, like our changing bodies; change thrust upon us, such as the death of someone close to us; and change we choose, such as the decision to reach a goal. During the course of our lifetime we can expect to experience all of these changes.

Once we were young and had the attributes of a child. Then we seemed to change overnight. Our bodies transformed. Our interests evolved. Our choice of friends varied.

When we passed the adolescent stage and became young adults, we married. Many aspects of our life were now different from when we were single. Then there was the day Dian's life changed in an instant; she became a widow. Later, she remarried and decided to have children, bringing more change to her life. And so it is with every passing day, something about our life changes. It may seem to us that nothing has really changed as cycles are repeated, but the time, spacing and form is always different. It is never the same summer or the same flower, or the same moment that it once was.

> *"The years teach much that the days never know."*
> *- Emerson*

For the most part, change is a normal aspect of our lives. Some changes are constant and inevitable, other changes occur randomly and still other changes involve making direct choices. Change can be temporary or permanent, complex or simple and happen quickly or slowly. Whatever the nature of change, it requires time, for only in time can change occur.

> *"To every thing there is a season, and a time to every purpose..."* - Ecclesiastes 3

Stages of Change - The 4 'A's

We recognize from observing the order of the natural world, that change follows a pattern, passing through various stages. Other factors may influence the end result, but under normal circumstances we expect certain things to happen, just as spring follows winter and morning follows night.

In a similar way, we go through specific stages when creating our own changes or managing imposed change. Stages give us the opportunity and the time to adjust to the change. Even when some aspect of our life suddenly becomes different, we need to experience these stages.

We are not alone in identifying four stages to creating and managing personal change. What we do offer is a simple, yet effective way to remember them, the 4 'A's: Awareness, Acceptance, Action and Achievement.

Stage 1: Awareness

Awareness is the first stage in making any kind of change. We need to become aware that we even want to make a change or reach a goal. We may feel dissatisfaction, uneasiness, or even outright fear and begin to question where our lives are headed. Another obvious sign that it is time to start thinking about change is when we exhibit destructive behavior towards ourselves or others. Or a sudden change thrust into our lives often compels us into the stage called awareness, our first stage towards managing change.

Stage 2: Acceptance

Acceptance is the second stage necessary for change. We need to come to a new understanding. We move beyond awareness and acknowledge within ourselves that we want something about our lives to be different. Until now we have only been going through the thinking process. Perhaps we even share with others what we plan to do. We may think and talk about it for quite some time, yet find we are not quite ready to take any action that would bring change about.

It is when we reach the stage of acceptance that we are willing to make a commitment to work towards the desired goal. The acceptance stage may be symbolized by something as simple as picking up the phone and making a call, as Dian did in her story. When we have reached the point of acceptance, we need to do something symbolic or ceremonial that says *I mean it*.

Stage 3: Action

Action is the third stage. Action is the only way we can show ourselves and others that we have made a commitment towards achieving a goal. Some goals we choose to set for ourselves may seem quite simple, others more complex involving careful long term planning. We might need a little or a lot of help to reach our goals. It is in the action stage that we realize how much the change will affect our lives. It is also when we experience our greatest discomfort toward making change. Whatever we call this feeling of resistance, doubt or hesitation, its real name is fear. It is at this point in the action stage that we learn to face and adapt to a future with a difference, for without action, there can be no change.

Stage 4: Achievement

Achievement marks the fourth and final step in the change process. When we have completed the necessary work and reached the desired goal, it's time for a pat on the back. At the same time, it is helpful to be aware there is a paradox to achievement. Normally, we feel the exhilaration of our accomplishment, or at the very least, the satisfaction of completing what we started. We feel pride, increased self-esteem and a sense of well being; in short, we feel good about ourselves, and so we should. Yet another part of us may feel let down. We might wonder whether it is normal to experience a conflict between feeling victorious while also feeling doubts. Our inner conflict reflects a natural aspect of the change process, and therefore a part of achieving goals. As long as we recognize the paradoxical nature of our feelings, the less likely we are to be caught unaware. Part of the achievement stage is in allowing ourselves time to adjust to our success.

Time and the Movement of Change

We also need to be aware that each stage of change requires its own movement through time. No set amount of time exists from the point when we first come to the stage of awareness to where we enter acceptance, move into action, and reach achievement. In fact, each stage may overlap with the next one for a period of adjustment.

Even when we establish goals that include timelines, there is a need for flexibility. This movement through the stages of change might be described as taking two steps forward and one step back. Yet if we continue to practice this dance, we will always reach our goal. We may not end up exactly where we intended on the dance floor, or we may even stumble a bit, but, nonetheless, we will feel the satisfaction of bringing change to our lives.

> *"You gain strength, courage and confidence by every experience in which you really stop to look fear in the face."* - Eleanor Roosevelt

Fear and Personal Change

Our reaction to the three kinds of personal change, whether natural, imposed or chosen, depends to a large extent on our past experiences. We learn there is little we can do about the first one, except perhaps to delay the advancing years by staying fit. We can do nothing about the second type, for these are the slings and arrows of outrageous fortune. But where there is choice one would think that change has met its match. Not so! For creating and managing personal change carries with it the unchecked baggage of fear.

Change always involves moving into some area of the unknown; otherwise it wouldn't be change. This unknown factor holds a certain degree of fear for everyone. It may range from the paralyzing fear that keeps us from any kind of movement to the opposite end of the spectrum, eliciting a feeling of excitement. We may turn from it; we may seek to embrace it; but rarely do we escape it, as we leave the reassuringly familiar for the scary unknown.

> *"Why are we scared to die? Do any of us remember being scared when we were born?"*
> \- Trevor Kay

From the Journals of SubContact: Natal Fear

I see a mountain with two crosses on top. I'm flying, as if in a helicopter and as I move closer I see that what I took to be crosses are really an array of antennae. There are two towers and each has a different configuration of devices. I want to have a better look at the mountain so I move back and I see that it stands pretty much apart from the neighboring hills. I move closer and land gently on my feet near the base of the two towers.

I have a feeling in some way that I cannot express that this is my mountain and that these are my antennae pointing this way and that – receiving, processing and sending data.

I begin to distinguish the difference between the two towers. The one on the left is older than the other one, although both of them have received additions and modifications over time. I have a strong intuition that the one on the left is directed towards the past and that the other points to the future. I also get the sense that these represent yin and yang and what small space there is between the two antennae represents the present, a place where I always am, whether I'm aware of it or not.

And there is more. To the left, which means my past, was my birth. To the right and forward will be my death. And along the way, as the earth turns and makes its orbits around the sun and the seasons change, what's important is this small slice of time in my here and now.

I see that what I first took as wires and cables is in reality a stylized serpent coiling around the antenna on the left. It occurs to me that the snake symbolizes unspoken fear, and I know the serpent is in the past, where the fear was, and here's the important part, it represents things that have already happened.

The fear that every person carries with them, and doesn't recognize, is the sheer terror of birth. It is knowing that outside the womb is a life all alone which is fearsome to behold. The womb was a place of the freedom of dependence. It was a place where we were immune from fear itself.

Some make the transition toward birth wanting no more than that first gasp of life. Some want to delay forever that first breath, because it means 'I'm alone'. Suddenly something happens, you are on your own, separate from the environment that was so familiar that you didn't want to leave it.

Nothing that describes the trauma of birth can be overstated. If anything is recorded in the book of our collective unconscious it is birth. Birth is also stamped in the memories of our DNA, although they'll never find the code under a microscope. Some people, because they cannot remember that helpless terror of birth, mistakenly believe that the hole inside of them that they can't identify is the fear of death. But it is the unremembered fear of birth. Both birth and death are a form of dying. To some people, the fear of living outweighs that of dying. The greatest fear for others is the fear of dying without completing that which is theirs to complete. For most people, more fearsome than death is the beginning of life.

The SubContact ends.

> **"Fear is that little darkroom where negatives are developed."** - Michael Pritchard

The Nature of Fear

Fear is our friend; it helps us survive. We easily recognize fear as the fight or flight reflex. Babies of all kinds, including humans, exhibit what researchers call innate fears. Classic studies into human infant behavior have concluded that babies are afraid of loud noises and falling. Loud noises seem reasonable when we consider that we spent the first months of our lives in a place where sound was muffled. Then when we were born, suddenly the volume got turned up.

On the other hand, fear of falling, which was demonstrated when babies refused to crawl onto a transparent tabletop past a point that appeared to have no support, may have an additional explanation. This experiment was said to sustain the theory that infants have an innate fear of falling. However, if babies were simply afraid of falling, how would they ever learn to walk? We might just as reasonably say that the infants were afraid of having a very scary looking experience.

Perhaps, in the very foundation of our being there is a time, now forgotten, when we experienced a terrifying change. A time when we were helplessly thrust from everything we knew that was familiar into a totally unknown environment.

It would seem we have already survived the greatest change life can bring us, our own birth. And despite the trauma of that experience, it is beyond our conscious recall. Yet fear persists in keeping many of us from achieving our goals and making changes. Fear has become one of our greatest self-imposed obstacles to change.

As a safeguard for our early years, fear ensured that we had the opportunity to develop and adapt to an ever-changing world. At the same time, with a healthy dose of curiosity and a reasonable amount of encouragement, we discovered some of our fears could be set aside and even forgotten as we learned new things. But what happens if we don't get the right encouragement to overcome our fears? Is it possible that we might get stuck in certain behaviors?

We know there are critical periods in our early lives that are dependent upon receiving adequate stimulation for healthy development, such as learning the use of language and speech. We would suggest that our emotional development has critical periods as well. There are recorded instances when infants died from what is attributed to a lack of intimacy and touching in old style orphanages. These toddlers were hardly ever picked up. Is it possible that, lacking reassuring touch, the fears of the infants became so overwhelming that they perished? It is hard to imagine such a self-destructive behavior given an organism's basic instinct for survival, but then babies have limited resources for expressing their feelings. It is in our early life that we begin to form the behaviors that help us cope with our fears.

Our fear-driven behavior easily becomes a conditioned or learned response that can automatically transfer to other situations. When that situation contains cues that remind us of a similar experience, we tend to react in the same way. In other words, we follow a pattern that successfully helps us cope with our fear. However, what we may have once perceived as a reasonable reaction may no longer serve us very well. In fact, it may do us greater harm than good. That is why we urge the examination of our fears. Then we can see if these fears are still useful to us or have become unidentified fears that stand as obstacles to change. We call this:

Looking for UF the Tragic Dragon

In the song *Puff the Magic Dragon* by Yarrow and Tipton, the lyrics tell of the relationship between the little boy and his fantasy friend, a dragon named Puff. When we get to the end of the song, we find that Jackie outgrows the need for his mythical playmate. Some people find this ending sad.

But what about UF the Tragic Dragon? UF stands for Unidentified Fears. Many of us carry UF with us well into adulthood, and even into old age. And what a dragon UF is, dictating to us and making demands that are no longer valid. That's what makes UF tragic.

We are particularly interested in Unidentified Fears, fears we carry over from our past experiences. When they keep us from engaging in positive change, or having new worthwhile experiences, they have become liabilities. How many times does our behavior cause us to say, "I'll never do that again"? Only to find that the next time, in a similar situation, we do it all over again. Our suggestion is to identify the fear that keeps us stuck in our maloopa and find ways to overcome it. Make a decision to send UF back to his cave!

> *"Fears are educated into us and can, if we wish, be educated out."* - Karl Menninger

The Generation Gap

A simple exercise to help us get used to the idea of recognizing fear is something we call the generation gap. To begin, we simply list as many words as we can that are related to the word f-e-a-r. At last count, we had a list of nearly one hundred and fifty words. That's almost twice as many words for fear as the Inuit have for snow. The practice of identifying different types of snow no doubt plays a role in the survival of Inuit, who live in Northern Canada. However, when we use euphemisms for fear we may be decreasing the quality of our survival by using words that disguise just how much fear is really present in our everyday lives. In effect, we're giving ourselves a snow job!

We have explained that life is naturally fearful, and that we are often manipulated by this emotion. The point we want to stress is that we are not generally aware of the extent to which fear is present. For example, let's take a word we use quite often, such as *worry,* and see where it leads us. To worry is to be anxious; to have anxiety is to be fearful. When we worry, then, we are afraid. We have closed the generation gap when we can take a word and recognize that it contains the face of fear. How about taking another word, such as *misgivings*. When we have misgivings we hesitate. When we hesitate we have doubts. To doubt something is often to be afraid of the truth. Once again we have closed the gap and found fear.

Let's examine the word - *discourage*. We all know what it feels like to be discouraged, but how many of us have examined the word closely? ***Dis – courage*** means literally to be robbed of courage. What pops into our mind when we describe someone who has no courage? We think that person is probably a coward, full of fear. But when we use the term *dis-couraged*, this tends to evoke some kind of weary-like malaise that has affected us, rather than a fear that we might fail. That shape-shifting coward, fear, once again takes cover behind our curtain of awareness.

By looking at just a few words that we routinely substitute for fear, we are able to trace them back to their family origin. Having closed the generation gap, we realize how unaware we have been of our intimate relationship with the offspring of fear.

A Simple Guide to Knowing Fear

When we, the authors, first met we were already convinced of the value of examining fears. Individually, we came to the awareness that we needed to change something about the way we were living. With that acceptance, each of us undertook a personal inventory that helped us identify our fears. This is a process we continue to rely on because we have learned that the many faces of fear, often subtly, become the motivating factor that can misdirect our choice of behaviors.

We explain in detail a four-step guideline for identifying our fears based on the model found in the original twelve-step program of Alcoholics Anonymous. Surveys of twelve-step participants show that they believe taking a personal inventory based on their fears is a primary ingredient towards making a successful life-change. It is our belief that this simple yet effortful process makes a tremendous difference in recognizing and challenging the fears that hide within.

Naming our fear often sets us free from that very fear. We can then turn our attention to creating and managing change.

Chances are that anyone who makes the effort to identify their own unreasoned fears will enjoy the same benefits as we describe. After all, there is nothing to lose but our fear.

> *"Ultimately we know deeply that the other side of fear is freedom."* - Marilyn Ferguson

Four Steps to Identifying Fear

To find our fears it is helpful, if not essential, to make a list of our past hurts. We need to be specific about this: who caused us to feel hurt and how did it affect our lives? Because of its importance, this exercise is something we will want to begin as soon as possible after we have read over the guidelines. Remember, this is part of our *Action* stage; we need to put ink to paper, fingers to keyboard to complete the steps of identifying our fears.

Step 1: Who?

Using a four column formula of who, why, how and what, we begin with the first column, *Who*. There are three areas that the hurt may have come from – *people*, *places* or *things*. People are the easiest to identify and we usually begin with our close family members.

Almost immediately, we can bring to mind an incident or two where we felt hurt by something that was said or done by mum, dad, sister, brother, aunt or uncle. In addition to our family, there are friends, teachers, past lovers and others that might have offended us. Once we begin it gets easier.

Places and *things* are a little more difficult to put our finger on. Places are organizations or institutions, such as a school, a church, a particular group, or something bigger, like a law enforcement agency or the tax department.

Things refer to principles, laws or ideas that may have originated with one of the places. For example, we have a law that states we must wear a seatbelt while travelling in a car. Some of us may feel resentful at being told that we must either do this or pay a fine if we get caught.

Another way to identify our hurts is to use the word resentment. When we remember our hurts we feel some degree of resentment. To resent means to relive negative feelings. When we remember our hurts and feel angry, we are reliving our fears. Resentment and anger are more words that hide our fear. We get angry because we are afraid, afraid that we might either lose something or fail to get what we want. This brings us to the second step.

Step 2: Why?

Why did we feel hurt? Was something said or done that hurt our feelings? The emphasis here is to remember the hurt in exactly our own words, then write it down. At first, when we begin the process, we feel some of the sting it caused us, which means we are resentful. Sometimes we might even get angry all over again. Good. That squirmy hidden fear just popped into our awareness. Keep the faith, because there's only one more step to go before we see it for what it really is. This is a good time to stop and consider the courage that it took us to get this far into our feelings. Remember the origin of dis-couraged, there's just a little farther to go.

Step 3: How?

Now we need to understand just *how* this hurt affects us. We look to identify the specific area in our personal life that was directly related to our feeling of hurt, anger or resentment. How was our sense of inner value involved; was it our self-esteem, self-worth, self-confidence, or any of the other self-words we use?

How was our feeling of pride affected? Did we feel slighted when it came to pride in our abilities, loved ones, culture or country? How reasonable, upon close examination, is our sense of indignation?

Then there are two areas in which our personal security may have been involved: financial and personal relationships. How did we stand to lose or gain? These are the areas in which we felt the threat of being humiliated, embarrassed, ashamed or guilty.

These are the feelings associated with our sense of self-value, pride and security, that are good indicators to identifying our fears and how they affect us.

Step 4: What?

What more do we need to know? Haven't we done enough by exposing these feelings? Not quite. Now we get to expose the fear that hides behind each source of hurt, resentment or anger. If we have been successful at making a list of who and why we felt hurt, and went on to describe how our personal lives were affected, now we can name what our fears are.

In the fourth and final column, next to the descriptors of self, pride or security, list a related fear. Here are a few of the names we can give them: fear of rejection; fear of being alone; fear of failure; and fear of the unknown. Or we might use words like: fear of being wrong; fear of not being accepted; fear of not being good enough; fear of making a fool of ourselves and fear of what others might think of us. This last one is a biggy, and can take different forms, but it really boils down to the fear of failure and rejection.

> **"Inferiority complex: a conviction by a jury of your fears."** - Unknown

When we see that fear of failure and rejection is related to feelings of guilt and shame from past hurts we come close to finding the source of how we formed our early perceptions about who we are. For example, we might have been hurt by *who:* a teacher; *why:* because she made us stand in the corner. It affected us *how:* our sense of self-worth and esteem.

We were *what:* humiliated in front of our classmates and felt the fear of failure and rejection.

It is these fears, shaped and formed through a child's lens of understanding, that helped establish our personal belief systems. These beliefs often keep us stuck in malaloopas, those harmful unwanted patterns of behavior that we repeat. For instance, what if our pattern of failure is really based on a fear of success? Success might raise the questions: how will our lives change? What will be expected of us now? And will we eventually fail anyway, so is it worth the effort? This brings us face to face with the fear of the unknown.

Similarly, consider a threat to our financial security. Money related fear might be based on how others regard us, our reputation and standing in the community, which boils down to the fear of rejection through failure.

When our hurts are related to intimate relationships, including sexual relations, we may feel humiliated or ashamed. Thus we may be afraid we are unworthy and will be rejected and feel the fear of being alone. These are a few examples of how malaloopas might have become a part of our lives.

Because we identify the underlying fears that created the pattern, we empower ourselves to change our behavior. We now have choices we didn't have before.

The Power of Understanding Our Fears

The ability to change the perceptions of our behavior is one of the benefits of understanding the *who, why, how* and *what* of our fears. When we make a list of our hurts we are better able to understand our personal history and we come to realize that we have an emotional attachment to fear.

When we increase our awareness of fear we recognize that the hurts of our past were often malformed because of a perceived threat to our inner self. We see that some of our behaviors became malaloopas, automatic reactions to those past fears that no longer serve their intended purpose. By identifying our fears we can know whether they are reliable as safeguards to our well being or emotional baggage impeding our progress. When we give fear a name we change our perception. In most cases, it liberates us. We are able to choose and adapt to change.

In some cases, especially if we do not feel liberated, we might want to share with someone else our discoveries about ourselves. However, we urge caution in this process, as time itself may be part of the solution.

In this first module, we have outlined a time-honored formula. We now have the tools to identify and understand our fears. Time and again, we turn to the concept of tracing our hurt feelings, resentments and anger to the root of our fear.

This four-step guide marks the beginning of our journey to self-knowledge. It prepares the way for further self-understanding through conscious contact with our subconscious. It is at this point that people of courage slap the face of fear. We have awakened in ourselves the power to explore the Unknown and experience the risk of change. We have already come a long way on our spiritual quest.

Concerning a Tragedy

The tragedy of the World Trade Center occurred while we were writing the final draft of this book. Like most people, we were deeply affected by these events, in fact such an event can cast a pall on our psyche. On the night of September 15, 2001, we had the following SubContact. We decided to include it because it demonstrates how SubContact can alter perspectives. As you will see, in the final analysis there are remarkable parallels between victim and perpetrator. Sometimes we attribute to our enemies immunity from regret.

Take comfort in the fact that, one way or another, the terrorists will never be free again. No matter what their ultimate fate, they will take with them the regret of underestimating the global and human response to their atrocities.

From the Journals of SubContact: Overhead Burden

I am underground, like deep in a neglected basement. I see a large pipe with a valve sticking out of it. There is a lot of dust and what looks like pieces of gravel all over the place, but most of all I feel the oppression from above, like something hanging over my head. What illumination there is seems random. Light seems to come from illogical places and to be shining on unlikely objects and at crazy angles.

As I proceed I have to keep my head down in some places. The ceiling seems to be of unpredictable height. Wherever I am, this place looks either abandoned or neglected. It's gloomy and there's a sense of impending doom. I also have the feeling many people waited here but now they've gone, like they gave up the ghost of waiting.

There are also some people still here but I can't see them, neither can anybody else, and they can't see me, but neither can anybody else.

I hear something - somebody just muttered something. I go in that direction, but continually need to retrace my steps because the path is not clear. I come out in what looks like a hallway. It seems strange, but it's as if I am in a shopping arcade that has been abandoned. Yet I see a battery-operated emergency light. It looks like it has fallen or been knocked over, and the light is pointing at nothing in particular, just skewed toward the ground.

I hear the soft voice again and it sounds like a sob. It came from nearby, perhaps around the next corner.

I see a black woman sitting on the ground with her back against what looks like a storefront. She's about thirty, wearing a white silk blouse and black slacks. It looks out of place, but there's a jaunty stylized turban pinned to her hair. Her legs look like they might be uncomfortable, one is straight out and she's sitting on the other one. I walk up to her and say, "Can I help you?"

She looks towards me and I can see that she has difficulty focusing. She says, "I'm beyond help. I'll soon be with God. I keep thinking about my son, Tyrell, he's eight."

"Perhaps I can help you if you tell me where we are."

"I'm not sure. All I know is I wasn't on this floor when the shaking started. We were all laughing and then something happened. We took too long to get out and then something happened again. Now I'm alone and I'm scared."

"You look uncomfortable. Can I help you to your feet?"

"No use. I haven't felt my legs for - how long's it been, anyway? Seems like forever."

I can see now that her back is broken, that's why she's propped up at such an awkward angle, she can't feel from the waist down.

"Are there others around?" I ask her.

"Not any more. There was a guy up a floor or two, but he stopped crying a while ago now. Then there was Edina. She... went away, too."

"Do you know the way out?" I asked her, "Maybe I can help you get out of here."

"I can't move. I just wish I could see Tyrell before I go."

"Is there any comfort I can give you?"

"Yeah," she said raising her hand feebly toward the tilted ceiling, "Take away all this stuff from bein' over my head."

Suddenly I am in the desert.

I see a large pipe with a valve sticking out of it. There's a lot of gravel around, but most of all I feel the oppression hanging over my head. What light there is seems randomly generated by the moon and stars.

As I proceed I feel I need to watch my head, yet I see nothing above me. This place looks isolated and neglected. It's gloomy and there's a sense of impending doom.

I hear something - somebody muttered something. I go in that direction but continually need to retrace my steps because the path is not clear. I come out to where it looks like there's a road. It seems strange and I wonder how I got here in the desert.

I hear a soft voice again and it sounds like a sob. It came from nearby, perhaps around the next corner.

I see a native man sitting on the ground with his back against a rock. He's about thirty, wearing Arab garb of a white shirt and pants and turban. He is just sitting there, not moving very much. I go to him and say, "Can I help you?"

He looks toward me and I can see tears blur his vision. "I'm beyond help, may Allah forgive me. If I could just see my daughter once more... Adeela."

"Perhaps I can help you if you tell me where we are."

"Once I was so sure - but now I doubt. When we were all together and we were all laughing, our shouting made us brave. Now I'm alone and I'm scared."

"You look uncomfortable. Can I help you to your feet?"

"There is no use now. I have lost my soul since we did what we did on that day. It seems like so long ago."

"Are there others nearby?"

"Not any more. I heard someone crying a while ago, but that was before I heard the shot."

"Do you know your way out?"

"I can't go anywhere. I just wish I could see Adeela before I'm taken from here."

"Is there any way I can help you?"

"Yes," he says pointing feebly to overhead, "Take away the vengeance that will come from the sky."

Someone from the other side is calling me. I find myself back in the gloomy basement.

The woman says to me, "I had to ask who you are that you can appear and disappear from this place and nobody else is able to."

I struggle with an answer, but before I can utter it, I see that she has passed on.

The SubContact ends.

Chapter 3

Module 2- Power Meditation

From the Journals of SubContact: The Unseen Arch

It looks strange to see the old man standing at the busy intersection of two broad boulevards. He is wearing a hooded robe, much like that of a monk and I recognize him from an earlier SubContact, he had said his name was Erasmus. I know he is waiting for me. He nods as I approach.

We stand there, watching people and cars come and go. We are in the center of noise and haste. The sound of shoes on concrete competes with the chatter of hurried conversation and the rumble of traffic. It is a hot day and pedestrians crowd the meager shady areas. Cars clamor to get out of the relentless sun, but there is no shade for them.

Erasmus asks me, "Do you see the serenity here?"

I look around but all I see is people and traffic in conflict. I say, "No, I see no such thing here."

"Look beyond the traffic."

I try to imagine what he means and look around again for any sign of calm. I see none and say to him, "How can there be serenity in such a place? The traffic is noisy and the pedestrians are preoccupied."

"When in chaos, you must learn to look for order. You are distracted by cars and their noise."

He waves his arm as if describing a far off hill - and the traffic disappears; it just ceases to be.

I remind myself that I am in a SubContact where nothing surprises me. But I am curious.

"Where did the traffic go?" I ask him.

He replies quietly, "It is there still, I've simply removed it from your awareness. Now can you see the serenity about you?"

I hear the sounds of people talking loudly, hurriedly, as if their words will disappear if they don't get them out quickly. And the constant scuffle of footfalls does not sound to me like tranquility. "No, sir," I reply, "I see and hear nothing but commotion."

Once again he sweeps his arm in an arc over the scene. Soundlessness descends but the hurried movement of the throng continues.

"There," he says, "perhaps now you can observe those who proceed in tranquility."

In the sudden silence I study the passing people once again. They make no sound although everything about them moves. It is eerie to experience a busy intersection filled with passing people who make no sound. I see smiles and sneers, laughs and leers, grins and grimaces, but I see nothing I would call serenity. I say so to my guide.

He smiles at me patiently. "Look for the unseen arch. There you will find people who walk in peace with themselves."

Once again I scan the crowd. There are those who trudge alone, but they do not look easy about it. There are those who walk in groups, but seem to wish they were elsewhere. Couples stroll in apparent contentment, but there is more lust and longing in their demeanor than serenity.

And then I see a woman, across the street, walking with two cohorts. I distinctly saw her emerge from beneath an arch that has now faded. There is a confidence about her stride, casualness about her demeanor and calmness in her eye. There is a woman who walks in peace.

And there, not 10 feet in front of me, an older man emerged from an archway, which then disappears. There is an unmistakable quality to his eyes that are like a window on his patient soul. He walks with untroubled bearing. As he passes me I look into his eyes and know this man has come to terms with fear and thus knows courage.

And there someone walks through an arch, and there.

I say to my guide, "Yes, I see some people with serenity."

He beckons me to follow him and in only a moment we are on a small hill looking over a concourse that extends for some distance. If it were not for the concrete paving, it would be like a meadow. There are many people on the promenade, each travelling in their own direction. And near the center of the concourse is an arch. It is not a huge arch, just big enough to allow one or two to pass through. But through the arch, on the other side of it, I can see grassy meadow, as if it is a doorway to somewhere more peaceful.

The vast majority of pedestrians seem heedless of the arch, yet it looks so inviting compared to the unyielding walkway. They labor on unaware that an easier, softer path is just a step away.

But some people know the arch is there and walk deliberately through it, and when they cross to the other side, shoulders straighten, eyes become more clear and gait is unencumbered.

"Why do most people avoid the arch?" I ask Erasmus.

"They know not that it is there."

"Then how do the others see it?"

"They do not so much see it as know its presence."

"But how?" I persist.

"Some are aware. Aware that when they look inward they can see better outward. And when they look outward, they can see better inward. Do we not understand our own actions from watching the actions of others?"

"By looking inward, do you mean meditation?"

"By looking out as well."

"But... "

My guide turns away from my question and, with me in tow, floats down the hill and returns to the intersection. Just as we are about to touch the sidewalk, we pass through an arch.

When I come out the other side, my guide is no longer with me. Down the street I see a young woman emerge from an arch. Our eyes meet as if in recognition, although we are strangers, and as we pass each other I know I have seen serenity.

The SubContact ends

Power Meditation

What is It?

All forms of meditation involve learning how to set aside our attention and go from one level of awareness to another. We meditate more easily when we achieve a state of relaxation. When we combine a relaxation technique, make a shift in our awareness and experience inner mental imaging we're on the threshold of Power Meditation. Power Meditation occurs when we add purpose - not just for stress reduction or maintaining a balanced life - but as part of a quest.

The nature of this quest could be physical, mental or spiritual. We might seek to have a better understanding of the world around us or to solve problems more creatively. Our search may be a spiritual one as we look within for greater self-understanding. Whatever motivates us to begin to meditate, the continued practice can bring us results we might once have only imagined.

> *"You don't strive for sameness, you strive for balance."* - Bear Bryant

The Benefits of Meditation

Most people believe meditation is a worthwhile activity, but only a small percentage of us engage in the practice. Yet meditation has been shown to yield such benefits as lowering blood pressure and allowing us to walk with serenity through the hustle and bustle of a demanding life. Evidence, such as the lifestyle studies of people with unusually long lives, suggests that the ability to successfully reduce stress is one of the keys to maintaining good physical, mental and spiritual health.

In Western society, the practice of meditation tends to conjure up images of mystics, martyrs and magicians. Many of us associate it with unfamiliar cultures that involve a kind of self-discipline that we are not prepared to undertake. Rarely do we consider the possibility that meditation can help us solve our problems, come to understand our selves better, or simply take us on a great adventure.

> *"Question with boldness even the existence of a God."* - Thomas Jefferson

Our history abounds with great thinkers, writers, artists and scientists who practiced some form of meditation. We know that such well-known figures as Socrates, the forefather of Western philosophy and reasoning, practiced a standing meditation. The artist Leonardo da Vinci gazed at clouds for inspiration, until scenes began to unfold within the landscape of his mind's eye. Albert Einstein practiced what he called thought experiments, a kind of meditation that involved mental imaging. It was during one of these thought experiments that he imagined himself riding a light beam through the heavens. This imagery led to his articulation of the special theory of relativity, a problem he had been working on for ten years. As Einstein turned to an inner mental image, his subconscious was able to present the problem from another perspective, a point of view he was able to comprehend. Although Einstein spoke in terms of using his imagination and intuition, it was the deliberate shift in awareness that prompted his speculative theory. When he went on such journeys, Einstein was able to leave the conscious world behind.

> *"Imagination is more important than knowledge."*
> - Einstein

Getting Started

Any one of us can learn to intentionally set aside our conscious awareness and have access to our subconscious mind while in a relaxed state. All we need is the will, some know-how and some practice.

We also need to remember that learning anything new takes time. If this sounds familiar it's because when we talked about change, we pointed out that change is all about time. Learning is another word for change. When we have learned something, permanent change takes place. Remember when we learned to ride a bike? At first we found the act difficult, but we kept trying. We got over our fears and eventually it became easier until it became second nature. We no longer had to think about what we were doing; we reached the point where learning - permanent change - had taken place.

It is a strange phenomenon that we overcome the initial fears we feel when facing the change process. Yet successfully overcoming this fear does not seem to eliminate it for the next time around. Every new situation brings with it the opportunity to slap the face of fear, especially if we make a point of remembering that we've been here before.

Fear Reviewed - UF the Tragic Dragon

In the first module, Change 101, we prepared for change by making a list of our fears. By doing this, we acknowledged that Unidentified Fear is an element of our thought process, especially when we decide to make change. We introduced you to UF the Tragic Dragon, which is the symbol of unidentified fear. UF often hides within our motivations for some of the decisions we make. Unlike its namesake Puff the Magic Dragon, who disappeared when the boy in the song grew up, UF stays with us always. Whenever we seek change, UF raises his homely head to defend his status quo.

This is an excellent opportunity to identify our fear-driven resistance to change.

UF provides the rationale that discourages us from beginning to learn how to meditate. This is something new, UF says. UF gives us access to an unlimited supply of excuses. UF is not ashamed to repeat old and corny rationales that worked in the past. For this reason, UF will come up with stuff. Stuff like 'We don't have the time,' or 'This will cost too much'. UF is also lazy and when threatened with the possibility of change we need to be alert for UF stuff like, 'It won't work anyway', or, 'It sounds like too much trouble'.

When we have an opportunity to make ecological change in our lives, UF or no UF, we can only come out winners in the end. What UF is all about is protecting us from fear of failure, what others might think of us and the fear of the Great Unknown. Much of what this book is about is not letting UF have his way. Now we are prepared to face his challenges.

If, after examining our fears, positive change is something we still do not want, let it be. That may be as close to a reason as some of us will ever get.

But be aware, UF will come another day.

> *"What lies behind us and what lies before us are small matter compared to what lies within us."*   - Emerson

How to Meditate

When embarking on any new adventure it is a good idea to find out a thing or two about where we're going. A little advance knowledge is another way of awakening awareness. It's a way of letting UF know we want change.

There are many suggestions on how to meditate, and we will want to try at least two or three methods, but the important place to start is in learning to relax our bodies. As we let go of the tension in our bodies, we can then shift our attention to some kind of mental focusing exercise, often referred to as the practice of mindfulness. Mental focusing is using a mantra, counting, observing our breathing, etc. Once we have acquired even a little skill with the meditative process, we can feel the difference. Our brain waves slow down, our breathing becomes calm and even and our heart and mind have a chance to escape from the constant stimulus of everyday living. Some people are satisfied with this state: a refreshing time-out that brings some mental and physical balance to our lives. It is certainly worth taking up the practice of meditating on this basis alone.

On the other hand, we may be adventurous enough to want more; we may want to experience what Einstein and others did. When they meditated, they saw, heard and felt the vividness of mental imagery.

"I shut my eyes in order to see." -Gaugin

Once we get used to the practice of a relaxing, focused kind of meditation, it is easier to introduce the aspect of imaging. Again, we need some idea of how to go about experiencing inner imagery. Some of us may experience mental imagery spontaneously, with little or no prompting. Others may find it helpful to follow a few suggestions. This practice is more readily accomplished through guided imagery where we follow the suggestions of a trusted guide until our own mental imaging begins.

Our images may range anywhere from fairly vivid to seemingly nonexistent. For most of us, our mental imaging ability lies somewhere in between these extremes. Everyone's ability to experience imaging improves with practice. But before we decide where our inner sensing capabilities fit on the scale, we need to understand exactly what we mean by mental imagery.

Sensory Mental Imagery

Mental imagery refers to the internal sensing of experiences that have no immediate outside source of stimulus. This is what we mean by 'seeing with the mind's eye', 'hearing with the mind's ear' and perceiving the senses of smell, taste, touch and movement within our mind. It is more correctly called *sensory mental imagery* because of the physical senses we experience within the mind. We use the shorter terms of mental imagery or imaging, keeping in mind that the terms refer to inner sensing. Some authors and materials might refer to visualization as a technique for mental imaging. This can lead to confusion as visualization suggests there is only one modality for mental imaging, and that is not the case. Some people 'hear' what's happening, others may feel or have a 'sense' of what's going on. The important thing is not the modality but the content of what we experience; for over time all the senses are enhanced. After all, when we dream our eyes are closed, so why should sensory modality even be important? The reason we spend time on this topic is so that we may know what to expect; we may expect to experience something. Period. We know that anyone, even those with a sensing impairment, can experience mental imagery.

Mental imagery is a natural phenomenon that occurs within all of us, yet we may not have considered it as such. When we move far enough into relaxation we fall asleep. In sleep we automatically go through stages of further relaxing, blocking out our conscious awareness, shutting down our motor reflexes and engaging in the activity of mental imaging. To sleep is to dream. Sleep researchers have demonstrated conclusively that we all dream, whether we remember or not. To dream is to experience mental imaging. This should answer any concerns we might have about our ability to experience mental imagery. There is no question about this - we can.

On the other hand, we might ask the question, 'Why do we dream?'

> *"There are as many reasons for dreaming as there are nights for sleeping."*
> *- Journals of SubContact*

Communicating with our Subconscious

Dreaming is an automatic process, something like the self-regulating of our heart rate, blood pressure, body temperature and other parts of the autonomic system. We only pay attention to these functions when there is a noticeable change from normal, which is a signal to us that something is different. Dreaming is also a natural function many of us don't pay much attention to, unless a dream is brought into our awareness. When we spontaneously remember a dream, or when we prompt ourselves to remember one, we are actively communicating from our inner awareness to our outer awareness through mental imagery. Our dreams provide the perfect opportunity to communicate - we can't talk back!

> *"We dream to remember to fulfill our destiny."*
> *- Journals of SubContact*

Our subconscious has sent us a message, something like a coded message in a bottle that we have discovered on the beach. If we follow this analogy, the subconscious might be compared to the body of water and the beach to our consciousness, where we spend two-thirds of our life. Dreaming occurs when we venture into the water during sleep and the message on the beach is the memory of that dream. Our subconscious consists of material that is beyond our awareness; it is submerged.

Our conscious minds are capable of an awareness of seven, plus or minus two, pieces of information. On the other hand, our subconscious knows everything there is to know about us. There is imbalance here. This is a potentially scary situation. Yet once material from our subconscious comes into consciousness, it is no longer unknown. That's the really scary part. What we don't know might become known, and we might not like it, especially if we have been ignoring all those unread messages that litter the beach of our consciousness.

Unless we suffer from mental illness, or use mood-altering drugs, we can trust ourselves to have our own best interests at heart. Our subconscious only gives us what we can handle, when we can handle it. When we remember mental imagery from a dream or a power meditation, we are offering ourselves the opportunity to communicate between our inner and outer awareness. The trouble is we don't always remember, and if we do, understanding this interaction may be difficult. The next module, Dream Language, is devoted to helping us understand the messages tossed up on the shores of our conscious awareness.

> *"The best way to make your dreams come true is to wake up."* - P. Valery

There is a Difference

As we describe it, the practice of Power Meditation and SubContact does not mean the same thing as philosophical or religious meditation. Neither of our modules has any philosophical or religious ambition. The purpose of accessing subconscious material is to bring greater physical, mental and spiritual understanding to the individual.

Sample Guided Imagery

We end this module with a sample of guided imagery. It reflects the different scripts that we have used over the years to achieve a state of relaxation and access our subconscious. In particular, it demonstrates our use of conscious confusion, a method designed to confound conscious awareness for the purpose of passing through the archway of our subconscious. Once the participant establishes a routine practice, his/her subconscious will offer helpful suggestions to facilitate the learning process.

See the module *SubContact* for a more detailed description of the meditative process. There we offer additional suggestions and illustrate conscious confusion in a sample meditation.

The Creative Tunnel

This is a very special meditation script. As you'll see, it is most appropriate to finding a new direction in your life or when you need to solve an important problem.

Imagine a gentle, soothing voice as you hear these words in your mind's ear. The pace should be s-l-o-w. Pause in appropriate places.

Take a moment, and allow your body to relax.

Imagine, as you walk along a country road, that there is something missing in the puzzle, a piece as yet unidentified that, when you find it, will allow you to proceed to the next stage of your journey. Think of this unknown factor as a group of words - a phrase. And as you walk along the road place this group of words in a compartment in your mind. Now begin to imagine your quest as a wordless concept, a symbol not yet named. And as you walk along the country road towards a bend, place the unspoken symbol into the same compartment that contains the phrase. Notice how the symbol and the phrase merge together and observe as the compartment becomes shapeless and transparent.

Allow this compartment to occupy the center of your mind. Notice how comfortably it rests there, in the middle of your mind, right behind your mind's eye, where you can easily see it. It will stay there for the remainder of your journey.

And as you walk effortlessly along the country road towards the foot of a mountain you begin to make out an opening, an archway that is the beginning of a long tunnel. You approach the archway and begin moving along the tunnel as if the floor is a gently moving carpet of air. You notice that the right side of the tunnel is finished of rough texture like white stucco. Cautiously you reach out your right hand to touch the surface as you continue walking effortlessly. You feel the roughness of it and experience it in the left side of your brain. You remember that logic and order come from the left side of your brain and you think about the purpose of rational and analytic thought and how sequence and objectivity has its place in your life. You let your right hand drop to your side and think about what you've just experienced and realize that a measure of logical direction entered the container in the center of your mind.

And as you strive effortlessly along the arched corridor you look across to the left side of the tunnel where you see that the left side is made of the softest black velvet. You reach your left hand out and let it touch the soft wall as you move effortlessly along, letting your hand remain in contact with the smooth texture. You experience the softness in the right side of your brain and it reminds you that intuition and creativity come from there. And as you think about the value of randomness, synthesis and wholeness you become aware that another form of energy is flowing into the center of your mind, just behind your mind's eye, where all things are known. As you let your left hand drop away from the velvet wall you experience, right in the center of your mind, a wonder at the powerful combination of intellect and intuition, of *the successive and the simultaneous, of the analytic and the holistic, of the left side and the right side of your mind.*

And as you glide along the arched corridor you decide to allow both hands to touch the walls at the same time, feeling the white stucco with your right hand and experiencing it in your left brain and sensing the black velvet with your left hand and knowing its texture in your right brain. You allow the two textures to merge and become one. And now, as you continue along effortlessly, you notice that somehow the textures have switched so that the black stucco is on the left wall and white clouds on the right wall. You experience the black stucco in the right side of your mind and the white velvet on the left side. You sense, at the center of your mind, that your creative abilities have been renewed and you are open to new ways of solving problems. Once again you allow your arms to fall to your sides as you begin to make out the light at the end of the tunnel.

As you approach the exit you place your hands together in front of you and feel the energy flow in a circle through your arms and through your mind. You are near the end of the tunnel now, and as you emerge into pure white light, as you open your hands, you see that you hold a gift.

You move to a grassy knoll where you sit down to open your gift. You realize that the true value of this gift will become more and more obvious to you with each passing hour. And as time passes you find that you are able to solve problems much more easily as you discover the true meaning of the gift of creativity.

Chapter 4

Module 3 - Dream Language

From the Journals of Subcontact: **Don Knotts**

I'm walking along a trail in the woods. This could be in 2 or 3 places - near Vancouver, or Calgary or Brisbane. I feel as if I should be jogging, but I'm feeling lazy and just walking. I come to a clearing and there's a red brick building that could have been a school at one time. The building is abandoned and as I walk across what once was the play yard I step on crumbled bricks that make a sandy soil, but there are no clues to where I am geographically. Now I'm walking in deep grass and I come to a hill and the trail goes deeper into the woods.

I reckon it's midday because the sun is directly overhead and the shadows are directly beneath the trees. When I come to a clearing, it is bright with sunshine. I'm in a deeper part of the woods now, but I can still see details clearly.

I catch a glimpse of someone out there, off the beaten path, out of the light and in the shadow of a big tree.

I call out, "You, there! You, out of the light."

There is no response and I'm curious and stumble through the bush toward the figure, feeling the extra pounds I've put on lately. As I approach I see it's a man, but that's all I know. He does not appear menacing, in fact on the contrary he looks quite docile. He's just standing there, leaning against the tree, and wearing a sweatshirt with the hood pulled over his head. I can't make out his features partly because his head is bowed. I circle around him for a better look. He has his head down like he's ashamed and for some reason this irritates me. When I have completed circling him and stand in front of him again I say with some annoyance, "Why do you behave with such shame?"

He hangs his head even lower and his bowed head and continued silence tell me he's even more ashamed because of what I said. His demeanor provokes me more so that I find myself getting quite agitated.

"You're easily ashamed, sir," I say to him. He says nothing in response.

"Why don't you tell me to go to hell, sir?" I shout at him. "Why don't you say something?"

Suddenly he throws his hood off. It's the skinny deputy guy, Don Knotts, grinning at me the way he does when he's just pulled off one of his zany plots. He slides one finger over the other, making the shaming motion in my direction.

"Are you telling me I should be ashamed of myself?" I ask him.

He shakes his head no. We might as well be playing charades for all the conversation I'm going to get out of this guy. When I say this he brightens even more and holds three fingers up, as if to signal, 'Three words. First word'.

He points to himself.

"Don," I say. He makes a 'keep coming' gesture.

"Don Knotts," I say.

He indicates I'm getting warm. He rubs his belly, which is quite rotund, not at all the way I remember the character.

I think about his name: Don Knotts.

"Don Knotts, Donnots, Do-nuts," I say, and he gets more excited, but obviously I don't have it yet.

"Do-nuts... Do nots," I shout, and he indicates I'm almost there.

"Don... don't not... don't knock... "

He is jumping gleefully at this, but asking for a little more.

"Don't knock... it. Don't knock it."

Don Knotts raises his arms in silent cheer but then sobers again when he sees my expression, which must appear to him to be puzzled, because I am.

"Don't knock what?" I ask him.

He grins again and rubs his belly like he did before.

"Don't knock... don't knock donuts? Don't knock a big belly?"

He slumps forward into the position he was in when I first accosted him.

"Shame. Don't be ashamed of a big belly?"

He smiles with his mouth open, the way only Don Knotts can.

I say to him, "Easy for you to say. I'm wearing this potbelly, you're not."

Immediately he makes another finger gesture, this one with the index finger sliding back and forth across the thumb, forming a miniature violin, which must mean I'm sounding like I feel sorry for myself.

"Wait a minute," *I say,* "hold on here. Are you saying that I behave as if I'm ashamed of myself for having a pot belly?"

Don Knotts nods vigorously.

"So your whole pantomime has been about how intolerant I am of others who demonstrate shame too easily, but I'm guilty of being ashamed of my own body?"

Don Knotts looks at me with his patented serious look, which is hilarious to everybody but himself, stuffs his thumbs in his belt and says, "Yup, you got it, pardner."

With that he turns and saunters away, seriously imitating the determined stride of a gunslinger. However, with the hood bobbing on the back of his thin cotton pullover, he reminds me more of an oversized rabbit.

"I heard that," *he yells as he disappears into the woods.*

The SubContact ends.

Dream Language

From the foregoing SubContact, it's easy to see the similarities between this type of guided meditation and a dream. It is also important to be aware that comprehending SubContact is precisely the same as that of understanding a dream, although wordplay generally occurs less frequently in SubContact. As we proceed through this chapter we will distinguish between language, symbols, metaphors and context to demonstrate how appropriate each one is to both dreams and SubContact.

Understanding Dreams

An exploration of the subconscious, and the explanation of SubContact, would be incomplete without reference to dream material. In this chapter we hope to awaken a new awareness about dreams. Dreams are made of 100% pure, unadulterated, 24 carat gold from our subconscious. Nothing can compare to the purity of a dream. Whereas SubContact and Power Meditation invariably contain gold nuggets, they are at the same time alloyed with conscious prejudices, fears and other ironies. But a dream is the one occasion when our subconscious can finally get a word in edgewise without fear of interruption, editing or prejudice.

As pure as dreams are, they are also obscure. For most people they remain so, but we have developed a simple checklist to make dreams and meditations easier to understand. Given the four simple steps we provide, most people find it fun to unravel at least portions of the mystery of their dreams. The more we practice these techniques the easier it gets. We have also found that it is unlikely that every nugget of every dream will shine in the light of comprehension.

"Dreams are the royal road to the unconscious."
    -   Sigmund Freud

"If dreams are the royal road then SubContact is the road paved with yellow brick."
    - Bob Benson

This part of the SubContact program is called Dream Language and it contains four easy-to-grasp elements. What is unique about our approach is the emphasis we place on each of the components. We also provide easy to follow examples.

The four dream elements are language, symbols, metaphors and context.

Dream Element 1: Language of the dream

Everybody we've ever encountered, with no exceptions, dreams in humorous expressions and phrases; wordplay that playwrights would die for. Much of this dream language is in puns, vernacular phrases and inventive descriptions. Dreams also yield elegance of phrase worthy of the Bard. It is easy to dismiss these descriptions as exaggerations. It is also easy to capture the magnificent wording of our own dreams when we know what to look for.

It is as if there is a wordsmith in our head, and we mean everyone's head, that is both idiot and savant. It is amazing to discover how much rich language we can uncover. Awareness, attention and effort at decoding reveals that the master wordsmith of our subconscious sends important messages that are right there in plain language, waiting to be found.

Here are some examples of wordplay that have come directly from people describing their dreams:

> **Taking pains.** A man felt that the elders of his church were behaving in an unconscionable way. In the dream, he was breaking stained glass windows, *taking panes*, to bring the wrong to their attention.

> **Aldermen.** A man felt that his fellow board members were being led to decisions by undue influence; that they were acting like wooden puppets, and in the dream they were called ***alder***men

Mental institution. A mature woman returned to college. Many of the rules of the school seemed zany and illogical. In her dream the college was a *mental institution*, an apt description for any school, but especially apt for one with silly rules.

Will power. A man, whose father had died intestate, dreamt that his father had no *will power* when he died.

Carried away. A young woman dreamt that a man she recently met threw her over his shoulder and took her out of her house. When she looked at the dream she realized what her friends meant when they said she was getting *carried away* with him.

Such examples of word cleverness in dreams occur across all social and educational levels. It is a rare dream indeed that does not yield some puns. In fact it is so rare, we dare say, we were simply not alert enough to apprehend it.

We emphasize the language of dreams not to entertain with witty puns but to point out the language style of our minds, our dream making machines. There is as much innocence to the language of dreams as there is cleverness, as much inappropriateness as there is aptness. It is as if the subconscious mind brilliantly misunderstands words and phrases, which paradoxically, it obviously does not. There is, in our dreams, word precision that almost suggests capriciousness. However, we should not mistake precision for frivolity. Our subconscious minds send us messages that do not distinguish between the slang and the scholarly. It says precisely what it has to say - no more and no less.

We profit from listening to the language of our dreams.

Dream Element 2: Symbols

Another important component of dreams is the symbols they portray. A dream symbol is like a diamond. It is a complex idea, expressed with brilliant facets of a single theme. Symbols are the hallmark of subconscious communications. We have learned to watch for our own personal symbols, realizing our subconscious has been accumulating them over our lifetime.

We have personally adopted what are to us two powerful symbols, the arch and the dragon. A fractal arch graces the cover of this book as well as our website, subcontact.com. The arch itself symbolizes an entranceway, entry to some new commitment or adventure. The fact that our stylized arch is made from a fractal symbolizes our effort to create order out of chaos; for the fractal demonstrates that part of chaos theory that suggests there is always order, no matter how chaotic a situation may appear.

There is another aspect to the arch. It is impossible to pass under an arch without also passing under its shadow. The shadow represents fear. This moment symbolizes the typical phase of doubt we experience whenever we make a new commitment.

The dragon, of course, is our symbol for unidentified fear. In this book, we discuss UF The Tragic Dragon. We are quite cognizant of the importance of symbols, and adopt them to exemplify goals.

As they relate to dreams, the symbols we dream about are precise representations of a complex idea. Although they are mined directly from our minds, they are delivered to us polished and cut to perfection.

Archetypes

C.G. Jung went to some lengths to define archetypes. For the sake of our readers, we offer the following definition: Archetypes are elements common to every human's experience that cannot be reduced any further. For example, the concept of mother is irreducible. When we encounter an archetype we respond to its energy, we resonate to the presence of an irreducible symbol. We discuss some of Jung's archetypes in the SubContact module.

As an example of a worldwide symbol, we'll look to the police officer. The cop is an authority figure regardless of the culture. If such a symbol appears in a dream we can look for meaning in the fact that an authority figure is cast in a role. What kind of police officer he or she is gives us a clue to the meaning of his/her presence. Is it a traffic cop or detective? A constable or a sergeant? Then there is the question of what the police officer is doing in the dream. Is he/she enforcing the law, restoring order, arresting someone or just standing around? Each of these reflects a different meaning and purpose to the dream. We are alert for universal symbols and determine what they mean to us. Later we will be discussing the *context* of your dream, which also has a bearing on interpretation of symbols.

> *"We surround ourselves with the images of ourselves."* - Ralph Waldo Emerson

By definition, anybody could have a cop appear in his or her dream; that's what makes it a universal sign. Each of our symbols is uniquely our own despite the fact that it may seem that some symbols appear to be universal. However, symbols also appear in our dreams that are of a more personal nature. Getting to understand personal symbols is not a daunting task, all it takes is effort to comprehend each of them as they occur. For example, one person might dream of sitting at a computer as a symbol of what they do every day. To someone else who is not familiar with computers, this might seem like sitting at a magic answer box but they don't have any questions to ask it. In these examples, the same symbol has completely different meanings; one person is bored, the other is challenged.

We are alert for anything in our dream that is a complex idea expressed in a simple way. This is the hallmark of a symbol, and a symbol is a hallmark of the subconscious. Time spent identifying these symbols is richly rewarding in understanding our dreams. Everybody's subconscious is capable of astonishing creativity.

Keep in mind that there are at least two meanings to a symbol. One meaning may be obvious, easy to understand, almost too simple to be the one and only interpretation. That's almost a tip-off that we need to dig a little more deeply into alternative meanings. It's in the nature of trying to understand messages from our subconscious that we sometimes get a little impatient. Why can't our subconscious be a little more plainspoken, we might ask? The only answer we've ever come up with is that it's trying it's best. That belief allows us to occasionally walk away from, if you'll pardon the pun, the impossible dream.

A representation is the final type of symbol to look for in dreams or mental imaging. A representation is like a minor symbol, a less complex idea that in itself can be a clue. A person in a dream whose personality or character is known to us is likely a representation of their most outstanding characteristic. If we have someone populate our dream, for example a notably happy person, then we can work on 'happy person' as the symbol. Representations are generally about people, and more specifically about those aspects of those people that are relevant to understanding the dream.

In the final analysis the people in our dreams are really about ourselves. On this subject, we believe that the notion of 'channeling' is all about symbols and representations of our own subconscious devising. It is easier to attribute wisdom as coming from outside sources rather than from our selves. Yet to know ourselves is to honor ourselves.

Dream Element 3: Metaphors

A metaphor is our dream or mental imaging condensed to one idea. It is the theme expressed in the dream such that when we reduce it down to one sentence, it conveys a message. When we learn to pare our dreams down to parables we are presented with information our subconscious wants us to have.

We remind ourselves never to underestimate the power of our dreams to create rich metaphors. As we have described earlier in Dream Language and Symbols, everybody's subconscious is capable of stunning feats of concise story telling. By way of illustration, here is an example of a dream recently submitted to our website, subcontact.com, for consultation:

> *A young woman in the Philippines dreamt that her family disapproved of her online relationship with a man she felt she loved but had met only once. He was from different racial stock and this concerned the family greatly, although the girl herself felt no such compunction. In the woman's dream the family members each grew large trees and plants, but she and her partner were allowed only a bonsai tree, and she felt stifled and frustrated about this. She felt that she was losing control of her life to others.*

The first thing we notice about this dream is the stunningly brilliant metaphor of the bonsai as it relates to this woman's life. By definition, *bon* means 'shallow pot' and *sai* is a miniature tree. Bonsais are not allowed to grow and expand naturally, but are pruned back to yield an appearance that fits the whim of the owner. Due to the shallowness of the container, there is no room to spread its roots and no means to distribute its seed. In spite of the love and attention bonsais receive, everything about their existence is controlled. In this dream, the *language* speaks of being *out of control,* the scintillating *symbol* is of a bonsai tree, and the *metaphor,* concisely stated, is that her family controls her relationship and does not want the romance to reach a state where propagation occurs.

In this particular dream, it was the powerful metaphor that provided the unmistakable message behind the dream. Revealing language also appeared in this dream as did the symbols of parents and lover. Even the context was significantly appropriate, but it was the metaphor that went to the heart of the dream.

"Myth is the public dream and dream is the private myth." - Joseph Campbell.

When we work for the summary statement of what happens in a dream - that's the metaphor.

Dream Element 4: Context

Context in understanding dreams relates to what else is going on and where. After looking at language, symbols and metaphors we can now investigate the setting of the dream, the context in which things occur. If the dream about the bonsai occurred in a bonsai garden, where all family members nurtured their own bonsai trees, that context would provide a completely different message than the actual dream does, wherein *the family members each grew large trees and plants*.

The 'where' is an important part of context. What is the prevailing cultural setting of the dream or mental imaging? Is it in a basement or an attic? Is it in the city or the country? Is there a historical timeframe: does it point to childhood or is it current? What is the atmosphere like? In what way do we get a fresh perspective from the context? What prejudices are stirred? What questions are we left to deal with?

It is impossible to talk about context without also asking the question, how do we feel about the dream? If we wake up feeling frightened or depressed, we pay particular attention to the context of the dream. Similarly, if the dream gives us a confirming feeling, one of elation, we look to the context to understand what we might be doing right.

Day Remnants or Residue

Day remnants frequently occur in dreams, meditations and SubContact. These are interjections in the dream that are seemingly irrelevant. We're less sure about that, and although we've found day remnants to be devilish in their disguise, we suggest that they have meaning in and of themselves.

For example, in a recent SubContact session, the bellboy from Philip Morris cigarettes suddenly appeared bawling, "Call For *Philip Mmoorr-rraaaiiisss!*"

For those of you who are not old enough to remember this refrain, it was a prominent radio commercial at one time. The bellboy is supposedly calling out the name of a guest in a hotel lobby for whom there is a phone call.

Bob stopped the boy and asked for the message.

The boy announced, "You have two blows coming" and disappeared.

Following the SubContact, this passage was isolated as having potentially great significance. There is a tendency when decoding subconscious material to give it predictive value. Such was the ominous nature of the words, "You have two blows coming" that we fell into this trap once again.

Having moved from coastal British Columbia to the Interior of the province, Bob had occasion to seek out a new family doctor. Bob has asthma and was feeling the symptoms more prominently than usual following the move.

"Do you smoke?" the new doc asked him.

"Only four cigarettes a day."

"One side of your bronchia is more congested than the other."

He had Bob blow into a device that measures lungpower. Bob bungled the first test and took a second.

Following this the doctor said, "I'd like you to get a chest X-ray."

As Bob and the new doctor said their farewells the doctor reminded him that he would either hear from him in two days or he would hear nothing, in which case everything was allright.

The SubContact we repeat here was that night.

When we analyzed this SubContact, we could not dismiss the foreboding nature of the phrase, "You have two blows coming." Was something going to happen to a family member? Was one of the blows related to the X-ray; was it lung cancer? We quietly speculated on what might be the significance of the omen and prepared ourselves.

The next day Bob suddenly recalled the name of his new physician; it was Dr. *Morris*. Only then did we piece together the significance of the 'message' itself. When blowing into the breath meter, Bob goofed. He let some of the air escape out the side of the mouthpiece. The doctor looked at it and pronounced that it was only 80% of normal for a male of Bob's age. Being a competitive individual and knowing that he was in good physical condition, Bob asked for a retrial. On the second occasion, he blew at 30% above the average for his cohort. Thus Bob had had *two blows coming* in Dr. *Morris*' office. All sense of foreboding disappeared and that portion of the SubContact was given the attention it deserved, but within the context of a day remnant.

There are two points to all this. One is that day remnants can hide in devilishly clever costumes that can divert our attention away from other relevant dream contents, which supports Freud's theory about the manifest content of dreams. On the other hand, there can be valuable material in day remnants in and of themselves. In this case, Bob's subconscious made a connection between Dr. *Morris*, Philip *Morris* cigarettes, *smoking,* a *bronchial* problem, the *lung capacity* test, two *blows,* the drama of awaiting the results of a *chest X-ray* and a *messenger* from radio commercial. In making these connections, Bob's subconscious drew on experiences spanning over 50 years.

Day remnants or residue is believed by some to be data that is not yet laid down in permanent memory. Whenever we apprehend such material we notice it almost always has some quirky characteristic to the subject matter, as if our memory is having difficulty categorizing it. It is well to specifically look for day remnants before deciding on the final interpretation of a dream or meditation.

What to do with Dream and SubContact Material

We've had a dream or a SubContact session, it was interesting and all that, so what do we do with it?

One of the reasons Dream Language is Chapter Four in this book and not Chapter One is to prepare for this moment. This chapter is preceded by chapters with such titles as Change 101, where we examine fears, and Power Meditation, where we seek to know ourselves and the world around us. We are now going to present and then analyze a SubContact session. We will do this by following our suggested guidelines as they appear in this chapter.

From the Journals of SubContact: The Cognoscenti

It is night and I am walking along a path in a forest. I cannot tell from the vegetation where I am, but sense I'm in Europe. The passage seems to wend its way endlessly without any sign of habitation. I am hurrying, apparently to attend some kind of rendezvous. Up ahead I see a large building made of stone. It's too small for a castle but could be an inn. As I approach the front of the building, I see there is a barn to the rear that for some reason makes me think of a knight's stable. There are perhaps four horse-drawn carriages outside the main building. I know this is my destination and walk through the arched entranceway. I have a feeling the era is around 1750.

A very large man comes toward me as I walk in. "M'sieu," he says respectfully, "you are expected. Please proceed to that door." He points to the top of the stairs where there are curtained French doors. I climb the steps and as I approach the door it swings open. I enter.

The room is surprisingly well illuminated. There is an unusual blue cast to it. It is a large room, unexpectedly comfortable looking in such rustic surroundings. Three men dressed as if for night travel are standing in front of a large, round oak table, apparently waiting for me. They move toward me with welcoming smiles.

The first man is a small Chinese, perhaps 50 years old. He grips my right hand in both of his and says, "Welcome, I am Fong Shu." He turns to a tall burly man and says, "This is Judah."

We shake hands with silent nods and I look into intelligent eyes.

"And this is Arnot," Fong Shu continues, and a portly man, balding and with a neatly trimmed beard offers his hand along with a smile, a bow and a respectful, "M'sieu."

Fong Shu gestures to a chair as we all take up positions and sit around the table. There follows a few moments of silence. I sense that I am being scrutinized, even as I examine each of them. At last the Oriental man speaks.

"A long time ago, 500 hundred years to be precise, four men met by chance in northeastern Italy. It was a time of great upheaval in the known world. This was the time when the great religions of the world met and clashed." As Fong Shu spoke, I sensed that he mentally ticked off what he said. "It was also a time when various technologies and cultures began to meet. The crossbow met the scimitar. Mongols met the Anglos. The crusades were underway."

I had never thought of these times before and now I realized what a momentous time in human history the middle of the 13th century was.

Judah leans forward, apparently he will take up the torch from here. "It was a time of great fear and envy, hatred and greed," He said somberly. "Misunderstandings became excuses for wars as nations sensed peril from the strangeness of their neighbors. Some societies excelled at buying and selling goods while others had superior weapons and strategies." Judah held out his palms as if to indicate inevitable results.

Arnot is shaking his head, eyes downcast as if in sympathy. "The clash of colors," he mutters.

I'm not sure I hear him correctly and I say, "Pardon me?"

"Forgive me, M'sieu," he continues with his eyes still downcast. "I see the clash of colors, the flags and banners struggling to be held higher. The strange sights and sounds and smells of foreign peoples, it must have been something." At last he raises his eyes to mine and asks, "Can you imagine the first smell of curry? or the sitar first heard? the curve of Arabian blade first seen? It must have been something."

I nod agreement, wondering where all this is leading.

"Four men met by chance," Fong Shu repeats, taking up the story once again. "There was a Jew, a Chinese, an Italian and an Englishman. They spoke of physical, mental and spiritual matters. They were especially gifted men. Despite their different backgrounds, they were remarkably of one mind. They agreed that tools and weapons would continue to improve, war is inevitable as long as boundaries exist, religious differences will persist, man can be inhuman to man and word of mouth was a poor storehouse for knowledge. In one magical night, when prejudice was suspended as if by the alignment of the stars, they came to one startling idea; they concluded that knowledge needs system," Fong Shu says.

Judah seemed eager to continue the tale. "By dawn an organization had been born," he said dramatically. "Their name became 'The Cognoscenti', meaning 'the highest knowers'. From this humble chance meeting came the power of scientific inquiry and the systematic means to record and disseminate it. It was a secret organization then and it is to this day. We are now some 16 people with hand picked hundreds in our employ. We have limitless resources, because of our ultimate mission," Judah said with quiet eagerness. He looked over to Arnot and nodded to him, asking him to continue.

The Frenchman is quiet for a moment, as if gathering his thoughts. His face darkens as he says, "About 150 years after the first meeting, in fact in the year 1402, there came to be... tension within the organization. You see, from the very start the ultimate goal of The Cognoscenti was to further the lot of mankind. We felt certain that science would enable us to do that. But there came a time, following certain monetary decisions, when the darker side of some members caused them to ... break away. We call them the 'Contrascenti', although you would know them by more foreboding names."

Judah indicates once more that he will carry on the message. "You see, sir, it comes down to the fact that we are about to enter a new era in social and technological advancement. Our intelligence apparatus points to a struggle to be the first to harness energy of unspeakable force, a power independent of the beast of burden. It comes from the process of heating water and controlling the vapors. It is not a matter of whether these fantastic events occur, but rather when."

I nod to him. I look at the other two and nod to them that I understand what they tell me. Maybe these guys are in 1750 or so, but I'm from the 20th Century and recognize the description of steam power.

On the matter of the Cognoscenti, it was naive of me to think other than that there was such an organization in the world. Secret societies have probably been in existence since time began, but this one is beyond my imagining in scope and power. That there was an evil breakaway group that copied the successes of the parent, without the integrity, was also understandable. There remained a burning question, and I asked it.

"Why do you tell me of these things?"

There is silence among the trio. Each looks to the other, but all gazes eventually dwell on Fong Shu, who says, "It's a little tricky, but we would like you to join us."

"Yes," Judah says quickly, too quickly, "that would give us an edge."

"You are quite sharp," Arnot adds hastily.

As I sit there, feeling nervous and inadequate in such company, I begin to sense something is wrong. I notice a shadow fall on the face of the Oriental. In spite of the illumination in the room, I then see the same darkness in the eyes of his colleagues.

Shadow! Darkness! Tricky! I repeat the words out loud. I suddenly realize these are not men of goodwill, they are from my Shadow side. These are the Contrascenti they themselves spoke of, recruiting me for some black scheme against the Cognoscenti. With this realization I stand up.

"Gentlemen," I say, "I see through your scheme. I will leave now."

The three men rise as a unit, as if to protest, but fall back, realizing argument would get them nowhere.

I go to the door, open it and look back at my hosts.

Are those smirks I see?

I descend the stairs two at a time and pay no attention to the man who originally greeted me at the door.

As I leave the inn and head for the road that got me here I see an older man in a hooded smock, like that of a friar, standing near the path. I recognize him as my mentor, Erasmus, and go up to him.

"Whew!" I said, "that was a close one."

He regards me seriously, although I think I see some amusement in his eyes.

"It is your own shadow you flee. We can learn much from our dark side. You would do well to ponder these events."

Pausing only to thrust something into my hand, he turns and disappears into the woods.

I open my palm and see a pearl.

I retrace my steps along the path until I come to the point I entered and...

Dream Language   71

The SubContact ends.

SubContact Analysis

We will now analyze this SubContact. The first element is language and we will keep a running interpretation to capture the essence of the linguistic material:

Running interpretation - Language

It is night... I'm in Europe... rendezvous... These words suggest that we are in France. The fact that it is night suggests that there may be Shadow material here.

The trail is *without any sign of habitation,* emphasizing that it is a new place for me.

an inn... a knight's stable... around 1750... This language suggests that we may have 'an in' to a 'knight's table' during this period.

The *'M'sieu,'* and the **French doors** confirm the location as France. From a linguistic point of view, France suggests a foreign, but not totally unfamiliar language. The fact that the doors are *curtained* adds a degree of mystery and intrigue, which is heightened by *... as I approach the door it swings open.*

The room... blue cast to it... Three men dressed as if for night travel... waiting for me. This is a strange room indeed. It is *blue;* it is *cast* with *men dressed for knight travel* welcoming me to a *roundtable,* which suggests equality among the participants. It is as if we are being prepared for a meeting of ancient origins. The phrase *night travel* again brings up the possibility of Shadow material.

The spokesman is a man from the mysterious East. The names of the people are close to plays on words. *Fong Shu* sounds similar to *Feng Shui* the Chinese system for the flow of *chi*. *Judah* sounds like Judas, which suggests possible treachery. *Arnot,* is literally *are not,* suggesting this person might not be what he appears.

The phrase *take up positions* suggests strategic maneuvering and *I am being scrutinized, even as I examine each of them* implies a period of deliberate sizing up, as if we're playing some sort of game.

There is not a great deal of Dream Language material in the next paragraph. The one phrase we isolate is *ticked off* in relation to *what he said.* There is a suggestion here that there is incongruence between Fong Shu's words and feelings. We will watch for confirmation of this fact as we proceed.

Judah speaks with emotion-charged words; *great fear and envy, hatred and greed... excuses for wars... nations sensed peril from the strangeness of their neighbors...* His gesture with the open palms indicates results that are better off not described, but felt nonetheless.

Arnot speaks passionately in the language of the senses: sight, smell, touch and sound. *"I see the clash of colors, the flags and banners struggling to be held higher. The strange sights and sounds and smells of foreign peoples... the first smell of curry... the sitar first heard... curve of Arabian blade first seen."*

In spite of the mystical origin of his name, Fong Shu is the one man of the group who uses logic. *"They spoke of physical, mental and spiritual matters... they were remarkably of one mind... They agreed that... they came to one startling idea... they concluded that knowledge needs system."* It may be significant that he is also the spokesperson.

There is more than pride that motivates Judah; he is dramatic in his presentation. Look at some of the language attributed to him: *Judah seemed eager to continue... an organization had been born," he said dramatically... From this humble chance meeting came the power of scientific inquiry... We have limitless resources.* All of these utterances are not simply power words; they contain emotion and conviction. As we examine the language of each of these characters, we feel that we are getting to know each of them.

Once again we notice that Arnot employs words that convey sensation. For example, he says: *"... tension within the organization... We felt certain that science would enable us to do that... you would know them by more foreboding names."*

There is a pattern emerging in their respective speech mannerisms. Listen to the drama as Judah says: "*we are about to enter a new era in social and technological advancement... a struggle to be the first to harness energy of unspeakable force... It is not a matter of whether these fantastic events occur, but rather when."* Now that we have a good grip on the various styles of speech, we will defer further analysis of this type of material to the *Metaphor* stage and stick to language here, keeping in mind that the language has helped set the stage for context.

There is nothing untoward in the first part of this section, nothing linguistically unusual. But once they begin to answer Bob's question, a certain dodginess enters the picture. *"It's a little tricky, but we would like you to join us."* Why is it tricky? Why the 'but'? Something is happening here that we don't quite follow. At the time Bob recalls this as being as if they were handing him a knife: *"that would give us an edge." "You are quite sharp."*

This was early in our exploration of SubContact. We had little or no experience with the Shadow side. As Bob said in the actual SubContact - he felt inadequate. Having twigged to the real source of this session, he reacted, not like a researcher, but as someone who has been fooled, and is also a little scared. In his rush to leave the room in the Sub-Contact, he does not ponder the meaning of the... *smirks I see,* but in retrospect, the smirks suggest that they are satisfied with the meeting.

As the SubContact session comes to a conclusion, we meet with a bit of humility. Here Bob thinks he's had a close scrape, as you can see from his comment of relief. But rather than providing sympathy, his mentor, Erasmus, looks at him with *some amusement in his eyes.*

Bob is told, in subtle language that *"It is your own shadow you flee."* In effect, then, he has been acting like he's afraid of his own shadow. Like a good mentor, Erasmus encourages Bob and tells him that all is not lost, *"We can learn much from our dark side. You would do well to ponder these events."*

And so concludes an examination of the SubContact session from a language point of view. There is good linguistic material in here, and it has been duly noted. Now we go to the second stage of the examination.

Symbols in the SubContact Session

As we mentioned earlier, symbols are defined as complex ideas that appear as a single image or idea. There are some outstanding symbols in this SubContact session:

An inn made of stone: The fact that it is made of stone means that it is a permanent structure. The inn suggests that it is a public building.

Curtained French doors that open automatically: A symbol of intrigue. The value of French doors is to see through them, but these doors are curtained.

Three men, a meeting room with round table: An arranged meeting with a group of equals, as suggested by the shape of the table.

A Chinese, a Jew and a Frenchman: The symbol here is the international nature of the group with three different races and religions.

Members of a secret society tell me a secret: This implies that I am important to them. The fact that they are secret means they are unknown to Bob, at least until now.

The secret society is flawed: Human greed has led to the Contrascenti.

This is a momentous time in history: New power is about to be unleashed.

I notice a shadow fall: Suddenly the illusion begins to fade.

My mentor is there: Something reliable appears.

I am given a pearl: I am left with a message of value.

As we review these more important symbols from the SubContact session we begin to see that they mark the progress of the story. As we reread the summary of symbols, we see the story encapsulated. The important point to understand about symbols is their power to say a great deal with one image and a great story with several symbols.

Metaphor in the SubContact Session

When we examine these patterns we see that Fong Shu represents Bob's *thinking* self, Arnot represents his *sensing* self and Judah represents his *feeling* self. There is one side not represented here, and that is the *intuiting* self, and when we look back over the transcript we see that that is Bob himself. For example, in the early part of the SubContact, phrases occur such as *sense I'm in Europe... I know this is my destination... I have a feeling the era is around 1750.* Then later... *I begin to sense something is wrong...,* so Bob is the intuitive aspect. But we must keep in mind that all of these characters and all of the characteristics are Bob's own. The spectrum of modalities - thinking, sensing, feeling and intuiting, as identified by Jung, are all represented in this Sub-Contact.

How can this session be reduced to one sentence? What is the metaphor? *Bob catches his Shadow trying to trick him into doing work for it, but Bob catches on and learns from the experience.*

Context of the SubContact Session

To establish context, we need to take one step back from the process. The SubContact occurs in a foreign, therefore unfamiliar country. The atmosphere of mystery and intrigue and suggestions of trickery confirm the Shadow content of the SubContact. As Bob leaves the meeting, his hosts smirk, which suggests that they accomplished what they set out to achieve, to establish a conscious relationship with his Shadow side. In other words, context would simply paraphrase the metaphor in the following way:

> ***During a guided meditation***, *Bob catches his Shadow trying to trick him into doing work for it, but Bob catches on and learns from the experience*

This restatement of the metaphor is important because it keeps things in perspective. This is a good time to remember that the interpretation is our own. Especially in the early days of analyzing SubContact material, there may be a tendency to misinterpret. The tendency is to provide a flattering or less discomforting spin the first few times around.

The Medium is the Message

The message that is contained in the pearl that Bob's mentor, Erasmus, gave to him is quite clear: Prior to this SubContact, Bob had been overlooking his Shadow side as a resource. The atmosphere of the SubContact confirms this: mystery, intrigue, trickery, and secret society.

Bob had experienced Shadow material prior to this, but it seems he was undervaluing the messages. In a metaphorical story in which the *bad guys*, making themselves out to be good guys, were trying to recruit Bob to work against the *bad guys* is a spy vs. spy story with twists and turns worthy of an espionage novel. That Bob's subconscious mind allowed it to play out the way it did tells us that there's something worth looking at here. Notice that the characters from Bob's Shadow side did not do any denying, in fact, they were a little sly and a little sheepish when found out. There was no evil intent in the SubContact, but there were revelations such that, in the final result, Bob's Shadow side effectively *did* recruit him. From this time forward he was a little less skittish about Shadow material, and often investigated when he noticed his Shadow's presence. The examination of material from a SubContact like this one presents an opportunity for us to shine the light on our character defects. We all have a Shadow side, and if we allow it to, it will help us to deal with our imperfections.

"If you are standing upright, don't worry if your shadow is crooked." - Anonymous

This was the first of a series of SubContact sessions, over a period of years, in which the Cognoscenti made an appearance. That the Cognoscenti is a figment of Bob's subconscious there can be no doubt. But we wonder about one thing: if it's not the Cognoscenti, then what *is* the name of the *highest knowers?* Such a global, extra-governmental organization exists in this world almost without question. And it also follows logically, human nature being what it is, that greed corrupted some of the members, who then formed the equivalent of the Contrascenti.

Please don't misunderstand. We do not claim there is an old society like the Cognoscenti *because Bob saw it in SubContact,* but because nature abhors a vacuum and secret power must exist somewhere, as does secret evil power. It is well to remember that this two-edged secret power exists in our own personal world of the psyche as well as the world at large.

To Bob's psyche, the appearance of the Contrascenti symbolized a new level of self-knowledge. He considers its appearance here and in occasional SubContact sessions, as a sign of progress.

In the foregoing we have provided simple guidelines to help understand dreams, SubContact or mental imagery. Dreams require more comprehension than they do interpretation. So look for and understand the language, symbols, metaphors and context of dreams. Remember day remnants. And as we marvel at the inventiveness of such material, we are also aware that we are reading a genuine message directly from our subconscious.

Chapter 5

Module 4 - 4th Dimension Thinking

From the Journals of SubContact: The Creativity Room

I am in a long passageway, dimly lit. A tall, thin old man precedes me and as we walk along I notice the light becomes brighter. I see now that we are in the hallway of a castle-like structure made of brick and mortar. It is quite bright now and I see we are approaching an entrance, an archway made of stone.

The old man stands aside to let me pass and I sense he has entered this portal many times. I find myself in a high domed gallery, beautifully decorated with paintings, tapestries and carvings on the wall. The lighting, whatever its source, is indirect; it seems to emanate from everywhere, even places where there should be silhouette. I notice there is no shadow here, but beyond, through another entranceway, I see darkness where you pass beneath.

Once inside, taking in the rich decor, I gather two things: that my companion, who just stands there, does not intend to speak, and that we are to wait. I walk slowly around the gallery taking in works of art, each of which demands the respect of time. I am looking at the color play on a large canvas when I sense the atmosphere change, like cool air coming from deep within the castle. I look around and see a figure standing there, watching me from beneath a friar's hood. I approach him, extending my hand as I do so, but he raises an arm and points to the shadowed entranceway. As I almost reach him, he glides after his own direction and I follow.

As the figure moves through the entranceway, for just the moment that it takes to pass under the shadow, he seems to disappear and then, when he reappears, he has transformed into a young man with long blond hair and wearing brilliantly colored garments. He looks like a Russian Cos-

sack dancer about to squat down and begin to kickstep, except there is no music and I see now that there is some question about his gender.

We are in a very long room, perhaps a hundred yards in length. It is as wide as a house and the ceiling is vaulted in what seems a random way, yielding unexpected angles. The lighting is colored and is subtle yet brilliant, with blues predominating in the immediate area, but farther down I see yellow and orange.

The person whirls on me and says, "Well, well, well, what have we here? Another aging man looking for the secret of creativity."

I would not deny being an aging man, but I say to him, "I seek nothing more than you're willing to show me."

He stares at me and I cannot read his expression. He laughs a little and says, "You just said 'he stares at me', you said it out loud. I heard you."

"Since you take exception, perhaps I should ask, who and what are you?"

"You sound like Scrooge," he says, then asks playfully, "Who - and what - do you think I am?"

"You are a representation from my subconscious. Are you androgynous? How should I refer to you other than 'he'? And why do you answer my questions with questions?"

Smiling, he says, "Why not answer questions with questions? Didn't you just do that? As to your other question, 'he' will do for now."

"You mimic me."

"Au contraire, mon ami! I am here to show you originality, not imitation."

"I would think originality is more than speaking French."

"Ah, mon cher, you are too awfully alert," he says in a teasing way, "Do I sense the presence of anxiety?"

"Only in that this is a new situation for me."

"Excellent!" he says, as if delighted with my discomfort, "New situations are to be relished. They provide new perspectives."

"Like in this room, I see constantly changing perspectives in here."

"And so you should. This is the Creativity Room."

"That's interesting, what makes it so?"

"Walk about and see for yourself, dear boy.' He hesitates for a moment, then says, "But you've been here before."

"It doesn't look familiar."

"But how does it feel?"

"Perhaps a little familiar, but only vaguely so."

"Your visits are so short," he says, pretending to be petulant.

"Does this room represent the place I come to when I seek a creative idea, or look for the answers to questions?"

"This room, yes. This part of this room, yes."

"You mean I venture no farther than where we stand?'

"A step or two, now and then," he laughs, "and then you flee."

"Flee to where?"

"To a safer place, where the juices flow less vigorously."

"I wouldn't consciously leave here, knowing that inspiration is nearby."

"Don't be too sure. Some who come here venture too far, tarry too long."

"And what harm could that do?"

"None, unless you value balance. Have you never noticed how eccentric the most creative people are? Haven't you yourself noticed that some of the most creative people seem to be gay? All homosexuals are not creative, but the most creative people may be so. It's the price that's paid."

"Hmmm. That sounds like a generality, a stereotype, a prejudice."

"Hmm indeed. Study your Leonardos, your Michelangelos, any of your outstandingly creative people. And then there's mental balance. Venture too far into this room and *you might come out a little out of whack, if you come out at all. But don't take my word for it, dear boy. Venture forth, venture forth,"* he urges, as he begins leading the way to where the light is the color of blueberries.

I am reluctant, but take a hesitant step. Then I take another. An image flashes in my mind, the solution to a question that has haunted me for years. My guide is three steps ahead of me, looking over his shoulder to see if I follow. I take another step and when I do I suddenly know for a certainty that I have been viewing the world through distorted lenses. I know that when I take one more step everything will come into focus.

Instantly my guide is by my side, hustling me back from where we came. "That's far enough for now," he says breathlessly, "Each step can cost you dearly. Be satisfied to know this place is here."

As if waking from a reverie, I notice that I'm rapidly losing track of my new worldview. I protest to him, "But you said others linger. I wasn't there for long and I wasn't very far into the room."

My guide looks back down the long room as if there is something there that he does not understand and greatly fears. "I'm not sure what happens when people venture farther in there. It's like some of them make some kind of deal I don't know about. And then they forget about what happened." He returns his gaze to me. "And then they change. Best let me be your creative one, right? Let me take the chances, dear boy. That's what I do."

He makes a dismissive gesture, "Now go!"

The SubContact ends.

4th Dimension Thinking

This chapter is as much about promise as it is about process; as much about prediction as it is about procedure. We feel it is important to know how creative thinking works so that we may become aware of 4th Dimension (4D) Thinking when it occurs. Even more importantly, foreseeing the evolution of 4D thinking, how might we as individuals take part in this progress?

In order to see clearly how human thinking has evolved, and just before we get into predicting future thinking techniques, let's review how various thinking processes have occurred over time. We're going to provide brief examples of types of human thought and break them down into stages. We call these stages dimensions because, as you'll see, the analogy is appropriate.

1st Dimension Thinking (1D)

It's very easy to describe 1st Dimension (1D) Thinking; it is marked by simple problem statements and solutions. History's first way of thinking was dominated by survival instincts and basic needs and wants. For example, "I am hungry and there is a chicken" is a problem statement in its simplest form with a solution implied. If there is simplicity to the quandary there is also something admirable about the directness of the resolution. Consideration is not squandered on whose chicken it might be, whether it is a laying chicken or not, what might be done with the feathers, how it shall be cooked, etc. This quality of deliberation is definitely at the level of the caveman, and only articulation distinguishes it from the product of a reptilian brain. Some people today, although admittedly very few, use 1D as their primary mode of problem solving. It is noteworthy that the limited response of 'fight or flight' is a classic example of 1D. There is primal emotion in this thinking modality, and the dominant motivator is fear.

We do not mean to suggest that limited problem solving skills was the lot of all people who lived in caves; for during these otherwise dark days wheels turned up, spears made their point and boomerangs led to the idea of golden retrievers. But by and large, thinking processes tended to be linear, or one-dimensional.

> *"Everything has been thought of before, but the problem is to think of it again."* - Unknown.

2nd Dimension Thinking (2D)

The power of human logic takes hold in 2D thinking. This is a vastly more efficient way to think than the first way because logic contributes cause and effect. Anticipating future events adds the second dimension to 2D. For example, going back to the previously condemned chicken, a smattering of foresight will tell us that the demised chicken is the very one that produced our breakfast yesterday in the form of an egg. *If* we eat that chicken *then* there will be no egg tomorrow. So we cast our eyes about for other likely food sources, having logically attributed to the chicken the status, not of just food, but of food provider.

We owe a great deal to the likes of Socrates, Plato and Aristotle, who formalized 2D thinking. This was a quantum leap forward over the primal ideation of their forefathers. 2D thinking dominates the world to this day and is the cornerstone of almost any judicial system. In logical thinking, reason prevails over emotion; impartiality rules. One problem here is that logic is processed through the filters of our own thoughts and feelings. Another shortcoming is that logic in and of itself can stifle new ideas.

> *"Someone who thinks logically provides a nice contrast to the real world."* - Unknown

But there is a bias to objectivity; it bars the illogical. Yet what in their time were apparently bizarre ideas yielded great progress. For example, in a flat world, it was a zany notion to sail west with the expectation that you would come back to where you started. There was also a time when it flew in the face of reason that a craft heavier than air could sustain its own weight in flight. Similarly, it was completely illogical that quartz, which vibrates at 32,768 times per second, should endear itself to watchmakers struggling with how to divvy up a day. But all of this was some time ago. As contradictory as it may seem, it was by challenging logic that these examples of inventiveness, and many more, occurred. There came restlessness for a better way than just the utilization of logic to solve problems and create new ideas.

3rd Dimension Thinking (3D)

Thinking in 3D is defined as the systematic generation of ideas to solve problems. In 3D thinking, we add the dimension of depth. During the 20th Century, a host of new techniques were devised to assist in creating something new, whether an invention or the solution to an old problem. There was more than a demand for new ideas; there was a need to systematize the ideation process itself.

Thus was born brainstorming, lateral and parallel thinking and several variants of these. What characterizes 3D is the manner in which a problem is analyzed. In a typical brainstorming session, a group of people get together to throw what comes to mind in the direction of a moderator, who writes these thoughts down on blackboard or flipchart to see what sticks. There is a difference between brainstorming and the creative process, however we will lump them together to make the point that this is the deliberate application of techniques which constitute a system of idea generation. 3D is a cognitive approach to problem solving in that the purpose, whether expressed or implied, is invariably to alter the perspective of the problem or its solver. The ideation system called into play varies, but the purpose remains constant to the goal of changing perception or, stated another way, *re - cognition.*

4th Dimension Thinking (4D)

Thinking in 4D contains all of the elements of 3D thinking plus some new material. Thinking in 4D specifically encourages contributions from our subconscious, the warehouse of all of our experiences, which imparts the fourth dimension of time. This is an exciting new method that yields not only fresh ideas but also solutions that are ecological to the problem solver, whether individual or group, corporate or private. 4D is best conducted in a manner similar to 3D but there are important differences.

> *"Man's mind once stretched by a new idea never regains its original dimensions."*
> - Oliver Wendell Holmes

Guidelines for 4D Thinking

1. **Articulate the problem question carefully.**

The problem statement is crucial to achieving an appropriate solution. The statement should be devoid of bias and state the heart of the matter that needs to be addressed. It is helpful to pose the question using the following phrase: *In what way can we...?* As we proceed through the exercise we may find it to our advantage to restate the problem question.

2. **Gather as much information as possible; overload on data.**

Our subconscious can handle anything and everything we can throw at it. It is like a sponge when it comes to information. Whether we know it or not, it is our subconscious that enables us to make sense out of all the complexities of our world. Our subconscious is the home of our belief system, as we discovered when we named our fears. In fact, stored in our subconscious is everything we have ever seen, felt, smelled, heard, tasted and felt. Everything. Every word we have ever read is somewhere there in our subconscious. So if we overload on data to prepare the way for a new idea, our subconscious will churn away at making sense of it all. When we let go and trust our subconscious, it can be the most influential friend we could ever dream of.

3. Apply any or all 3D techniques.

There is great value in approaching a problem using a new perspective. New perspectives are the purpose of 3D-style idea generation. One excellent 3D method is to impose a randomly selected PO word on the problem statement. We'll describe PO later in this chapter. It is also helpful to twist and contort the approach to the problem so that it can be examined from several different aspects. This is where the book "108 Ways to Get a Bright Idea" will come in handy; it is a very good resource for altering perspectives. Here's the opportunity for non-conformity and freedom from restraint, so let fly.

Then

4. PURGE the obvious solutions

We wouldn't be looking for new ideas if the obvious solutions would do, so they need to be identified and set aside. For the time being, make a list all of the routine answers, but keep the list. In the final phase something in the new material and something in the standard ideas may fit well together.

5. Apply the concepts of SubContact.

We always emphasize the importance of pausing frequently in our search for an answer. This is what we call Dolphinizing, which is described later in this chapter. We've found it pays off to be patient while the most marvelous thinking device in the universe goes to work. This is also the time to be alert for subconscious material when it does present itself. As we know by our dreams, the subconscious can be pretty bizarre, so we're alert for the unusual.

6. Once you find 'the answer', go one step farther.

There are two reasons for this maxim. The first is, as Emile Chartier once said:

"Nothing is more dangerous than an idea, when it is the only one you have".

The second is that any idea can be improved upon. That being the case, why not improve upon it now? Often the brilliance of a fresh concept can blind us to its shortcomings. Once again, as in Dolphinizing, a pause is a good thing to apply to an idea you feel right about. Sleep - and dream - on it.

7. Do not skimp on Step 4.

If we don't come up with a good idea it may be that we're not using our most valuable resource. Our subconscious will generally provide us with the kind of answer we're looking for. If that is not the case, we've found it's worthwhile to start over, this time beginning with a Power Meditation. We take our problem statement and even a new PO word into the meditation with us.

Future Thinking Techniques

It's not that our crystal ball is clearer than that of others, it's just that on some issues we're the authority. That's certainly the case with the deliberate use of the subconscious and 4D Thinking. It is the theme of this chapter that a good working relationship with our subconscious will lead to greater problem solving skills. We will demonstrate that (a) the most brilliant, complex ideas originate from the subconscious, and (b) that the more alert we are to subconscious material, the greater we increase our chances of creating great ideas or solving problems.

The history of ideas is overflowing with stories of spontaneous solutions to vexing problems. One glittering account, that of Archimedes in the third century BC, has him getting into a bath, thinking nothing but clean thoughts, when the idea of displacement of water by gold hits him like a ton of bricks. He shouts, "Eureka".

Similarly, Friedrich von Stradonitz was climbing on a bus when he suddenly had an image of a snake biting its own tail and chasing itself on a pinwheel. Thus he was shown symbolically the circular nature of the benzene ring, something he had been trying to understand for a long time. The history of creative ideas is replete with similar accounts of flashes of insight. Invariably, these solutions occur suddenly, unexpectedly, from out of the blue and usually in the form of a symbol.

The history of thinking shows us that it's necessary to turn off the logic of 2D thinking in order to proceed to the 3D level. In the same way, at some point in problem solving, it is necessary to bring a halt to systematic idea generation and allow our subconscious to come up with the answers. This is the process in 4D Thinking we call Dolphinizing. The following SubContact session demonstrates this process.

PO - Foreword to this SubContact

In order to fully appreciate the following SubContact session, the reader should be aware of the practice of PO (Provocative Operation). Edward de Bono coined the phrase and applied it to the creative process. In de Bono's version, PO is the random selection of a word from a dictionary and the arbitrary imposition of that word upon the problem statement. Despite, or perhaps because of its complete irrelevance, PO acts as a catalyst. For further explanations of the original PO, readers are directed to almost any book on creativity by de Bono.

We have improved on the original process by including symbols and / or phrases to what is arbitrarily imposed onto the problem statement.

The PO word selected at random for this experiment in brainstorming in SubContact was 'legbreak', which is a cricket term previously unknown to us, which is allright.

This session is also an excellent example of Dolphinizing, a technique we have devised to allow time for the inspiration to come. Dolphinizing is the deliberate suspension of idea generation for a period of time. In a brainstorming group setting, Dolphinizing is exercised when the person, who is verbalizing a series of ideas stops and someone else takes over where that person left off. Individuals working alone can simply pause from time to time, whenever they feel the need.

Please join us now as we demonstrate spontaneous brainstorming, SubContact style.

From the Journals of SubContact: Break a Leg

I am standing outside what looks like a community arena, where hockey or basketball is played. As I reach for the door, my guide tells me the PO word is 'legbreak' which is to be applied to the problem statement, "In what way can we promote our business?"

I enter at the concourse level and walk through the first spectator archway I find. As I stand at the top, looking down at the playing surface, I see that the rest of the arena is dark, but at center ice, or mid-court, the spotlights shine on a set of tables set up in a horseshoe pattern. My SubContact guide is just outside the semicircle of people, standing beside a large flip chart on a tripod. She looks bright and ready, armed with two marker pens.

I presume I am to enter the horseshoe and conduct this brainstorming session, so wish me luck. As I go down the stairs, passing rows of empty seats, I notice there are perhaps 15 men and women sitting at the table on the playing surface. At first glance I would say they range in age from mid-20s to 65.

I reach the level of the rink and look around at the people as I walk inside the length of the horseshoe. I say to the group, "We'll assume everybody understands that the PO word is 'legbreak'. Who'd like to start?"

A young woman near the top of the curve of the horseshoe stands up. She's about 25 with long brown hair over her shoulders.

"When I think of 'legbreak' I think of 'break a leg', which means good luck in show business. In show business you need a cast of people to wish you to break a leg. And if you literally do break a leg you'll also need a cast. A cast supports you in the theater as well as in the hospital. So a cast is support, practical assistance to help you get your breaks. And when the cast wishes you to break a leg they also mean for you to strive, to make the effort, to go for broke."

With that she sits down. I notice my guide is writing furiously and I allow a moment or two for her to catch up.

An older woman, slim and short, about mid-fifties, stands up.

"When I think of a broken leg I think of a chicken leg, and I think of eating, tearing a chicken apart, breaking the joints and then eating the leg of the chicken. Chicken is also a word for fearfulness, timidity. And when I think of that I think of what if you broke your leg or were otherwise impaired from carrying on business. In other words, be careful in what you do in business as well as what you do to your physical body. Be careful, but don't be chicken about it."

She nods to my guide, who is still writing, and sits down.

A heavyset man, about 40 stands up and says, "Well, she certainly gave us some food for thought (there are muffled chuckles around the table). Anyway, being chicken makes me think of the need to put something on the table, to be upfront about things. Which leads me to courage; having the balls to take a chance. So together they make chicken balls, which is either an oxymoron or the name of a Chinese dish, or both (more giggling). And when I think of a Chinese chicken dish I think of chicken egg foo yung, which reminds me that you can't make an omelet without breaking some eggs. So, who wants to get cracking on that one?"

He sits down. My guide is writing as quickly as possible and drawing lines connecting key words.

A younger man, balding, early thirties, stands up.

"I'll take a crack at it and start with cracking open a fortune cookie, which often foretells good luck. I'm reminded that luck is often a matter of making your own breaks. Another kind of message when you crack a fortune cookie is wise words. In this case, that would probably be described as wisecracks (chuckles). Someone said, 'Luck favors the prepared mind'. That's an axiom, and axiom takes me to ax, which leads me to chop. All of a sudden I'm back to Chinese. You eat Chinese food with chopsticks. Another meaning of chop in Chinese is a personal chop, a sort of personal logo, a three-dimensional stamp-sized carving in wood. And the logic of logos takes me to a corporate symbol, or in this case a personal brand so that you can leave a three dimensional, sort of deep impression on your clients. That leads me...."

"Eureka," shouts my guide excitedly. "That's it! Three-dimensional business cards! Something to make people remember us. Holographic!" my guide bubbles with enthusiasm, drawing connections between keywords on the flipchart and drawing a circle around the bottom word: 'holographic.'

The audience claps, as much for their own teamwork as for my Guide's enthusiasm.

The SubContact ends.

This SubContact occurred in 1993 and as a result of it we went in search of holographic business cards. We could find no suppliers in Western Canada and eventually discovered a printer in Chicago. In the shipment he included about six different holographic effects. Friends and clients invariably rave about the cards; they make a lasting impression. Our company name proudly floats on a three-dimensional rectangle of ice and fire. Even at this writing, holographic business cards are a rarity. They are extremely effective if your intention is to add dimension to your first impression.

Venturing Farther into 4D Thinking

The most important advances in future thinking will come from two areas: (a) improved access to subconscious human thought and (b) the combination of technology and the expanding record of human knowledge and experience.

SubContact, while it is still in its infancy, is an improvement over 3D Thinking. The techniques we describe in this book, and particularly the chapter on SubContact, demonstrate that our subconscious is accessible providing we take certain steps. The first of these steps is to be ready and willing to accept subconscious material. When we follow our modular program, the most important step of which is to identify our fears, we are well on our way to establishing a rich relationship with our subconscious. The second step is to recognize when we have received a message from our subconscious. This is crucial, and to illustrate its value, let's do an instant replay as von Stradonitz starts to clamber aboard the bus.

Suddenly an image occurs in front of his mind's eye, a bizarre image of a snake eating its tail while performing pinwheels. How easy it would be to dismiss this image, chastise oneself for having such weird stuff going around in our head, and continue on with our day. But von Stradonitz was a scientist and many scientists allow theories to percolate in the back of their minds. Given such a practice, it would have been obtuse of von Stradonitz not to recognize a symbol when he saw one.

Many of us take a different point of view and are likely to dismiss such imaginings as a flashback from a childhood trauma or some such. Remember that Louis Pasteur once said:

"Chance favors the prepared mind."

There can be little doubt that he was referring to the emergence of subconscious material when he said those words. We learn to recognize such material and then to be prepared to put it to work on our problem, for the answers are rarely complete without the application of conscious effort. For example, von Stradonitz had his symbol, but he still had to figure out exactly how it related to his problem. He had to bridge the gap between spinning snake and spinning atoms by understanding subconscious symbols.

To summarize, we are prepared, having examined our fears, to accept rather than reject our subconscious material. Most of us have been in the habit of suppressing such ideation because we relate it to fear. But now we have had a good look at our fears, so it is safe to invite our subconscious to help us do the things we want to do. We have the tools to decode the SubContact materials as described in Dream Language.

As we said earlier, the second area of improvement in human thinking will emerge from the combination of technology and the record of human knowledge and experience. By this we mean all things that are written, handed down, recorded or otherwise made accessible to future generations. The perfect example of learning from generations that have gone before us is that we do not have to reinvent the wheel.

There are many excellent books out there devoted to idea generation and/or the creative process. Anyone looking for a good book on the subject can try almost anything written by Edward de Bono. Roger von Oech has written a couple of interesting handbooks. We also highly recommend a small compendium of idea generators to be found in "108 Ways to Get a Bright Idea" by Arthur B. VanGundy.

The Collective Unconscious and the Internet

Books and other recorded knowledge are one thing, but the Internet provides a whole new repository for human knowledge. More specifically than just the Internet, we predict that search engines like Google will, in time, become the electronic equivalent of the collective unconscious. At this writing, Google is approaching two billion in the number of web pages it can access. This is the collective knowledge of an enormous number of people, each of whom is reaching out to share what they know, what they do, what their interests are, etc. The shadow is there, the trickster, the hero, all of the Jungian archetypes that make up his concept of the human psyche are there to see on the web pages of the world.

Not only have we seen this progress disclosed in Sub-Contact sessions, but also simple extrapolation reveals the undeniable: the collective unconscious is out there, a point and click away. Of course, we cannot predict whether it will specifically be Google that will maintain its edge in this searchable knowledge base, but as of now it is head and shoulders above the billboard-laden others. In any event, one day we will all look back and realize that Google is the granddaddy of the electronic collective subconscious.

As for the Internet itself, it has become the closest thing we have to computer generated creativity. As the Internet evolves, what a wonderful opportunity we have to explore human experience. The searchability of the Internet makes it a coming power in human thought. Look upon it as an artificial collective unconscious, because if it is not there yet, and we suggest it is, it will soon have that power.

Brainstorming

We have talked to many people who are disillusioned with the brainstorming process. Brainstorming is only as good as the techniques employed. It will just not do for someone to act as a moderator in a group, spell out all the usual rules, emphasizing such homilies as 'withhold judgment', and expect people to come up with something fresh and new. The entire procedure is disrespectful of the most powerful idea machine that ever existed: the subconscious.

Read again the 'Break a Leg' SubContact as reproduced above. Notice the humor that is evident, keeping in mind that humor is essential to the creative process. Observe the flow of ideas as they move from one person to another. Take note of the almost subliminal presence of the moderator, who is only noticed at all because she is recording the bountiful product of the session. Note well the abundance of wordplay, a distinct hallmark of the subconscious (see Dream Language). There are camaraderie and good feelings among the people; they chuckle; they clap. There is no repetitiveness about this brainstorming session; it is like a well-oiled machine that just loves to produce powerful ideas. And remember, this one was done in SubContact.

For us, the practice of SubContact is a self-evolving process. It has led us to improvements in our brainstorming procedures. These techniques have been well honed now and have been found to work well even with a group of people who are strangers to each other.

The Creative Process and Practice

Like almost anything else, the more we practice creative techniques, the more competent we become. We have demonstrated that we can take the best of 3D thinking and combine it with 4D thinking to produce better ideas, concepts, products and procedures.

Creativity and Balance

It's great to be able to find new solutions to old problems, or to come up with fresh ideas when they're needed.

Idea generation is a powerful tool and the person who practices it invariably gets proficient. Like everything else in life, balance is required. For example, it is not always necessary to go to such lengths in idea generation that we are creating that which already exists. Often a new twist on an old idea is all that's required and thumbing through books or clicking through web pages will often provide the angle, twist or spin we're looking for. It's an old adage, but one that we practice; try to avoid reinventing the wheel.

We also mention balance in creativity because of the message that seemed to have been contained in the SubContact session that opens this chapter. The message seems to be a warning: don't go too far into the Creativity Room. But if there's a warning there's also a solution offered in that the character in the SubContact said, "*Let me take the chances, dear boy. That's what I do.*" We perceived a warning and took it seriously. We are aware of the need for balance in our lives, and strive to maintain such equilibrium.

PMI - Removing Emotions from Yes - No Decisions

The P.M.I. is a method of taking the emotions out of making a yes - no decision. Edward de Bono originated this method, and a further description can be found in several of his books. We're not certain that de Bono intended this process specifically to take the emotion out of binary decision making, but that is where we have found the technique to be most useful.

It is important to remember that we are recommending this technique for difficult decisions that arise, and where the answer is either this or that (binary; yes or no).

1. After you have finished gathering all information relevant to the decision, state the question in a format that can be answered with a Yes or No. Be sure there is no prejudice in the question, e.g.

> *Should I move across the continent to the wonderful city of Rochester?*

would be better stated as:

> *Should I take the job offer in Rochester?*

2. Establish 3 columns:
   Mark the first column Plus (P), the second column Minus (M) and the third column Interesting (I).

3. Enlist others to help you, e.g. family, friends, or role-play from alternate perspectives.

4. Generate and write down all of the suggested solutions or idea statements. You can start with any column, then move on to any other. The closer you are to completing the columns, the more likely you are to be jumping from one to the other.

5. Look at the Minus column, and identify the Fear behind each comment listed there. Refer to the Four-Step Guide in Chapter 2.

6. The Interesting column should have at least half the entries of the other columns. This is sometimes a tough one to figure out, but comments in the Interesting column are usually a spin-off from the Plus or Minus columns. Once you identify an Interesting item, you have the potential to change the problem statement. In the same problem statement example of moving to Rochester, for example, you might enter "HQ of ABC Company is there. Possibility of entering this field - my first love."

7. Take a nap or a break. Leave the question to stew in your subconscious. Sleep on it. Come back and review the PMI.

8. If you haven't already done so, and if you're ready, make your decision.

9. How does it feel? If it feels good, it is the 'right' decision for you, despite what anyone else might say is 'right' for you.

10. If you are not completely ready to make a decision then your decision may be 'no decision', which is a legitimate decision in itself. Whenever you feel like it, revisit the entire procedure, including the problem statement.

11. If the doubt comes back, remember how you felt when you first made your decision!

Summary of 4th Dimension Thinking

The history of human thinking has progressed from primal to logical to systematically creative. History shows that as these thinking styles evolved, humanity experienced a greater freedom of the human spirit. The future of human thinking will employ techniques to more reliably capture products from the subconscious. Capturing products from the subconscious is the definition of SubContact. The enhancement of the human spirit is the same as spiritual growth. Spiritual growth is the purpose of this book.

"Creativity is the power to connect the seemingly unconnected." - William Plomer

Imagination is more important than knowledge. Knowledge is limited. Imagination encircles the world
    - Albert Einstein

Chapter 6

Module 5 - SubContact

From the Journals of SubContact: The Cognoscenti Revisited

I am walking down a narrow cobblestone street lined with shops. It looks to be a European town just after the war. My intuition tells me it's about 1948. The street goes downhill now, but there is a bend in the road where it looks level. There is a small man walking several yards in front of me. He looks like he might be Oriental. As he reaches the bend in the street he looks back, and although I'm not far away, he seems not to see me.

As I round the bend and pass a teashop, I see the man standing in the doorway, as if he's looking at the goods in the window, but I have a strong feeling he's checking to see if anyone is following him. I stop and watch him and determine that he is Chinese. He is wearing a western business suit and tie but carries no attaché case. It is obvious he does not know of my presence.

After a few moments he resumes his journey, passing so close to me that I feel the stir of air as he goes by. He is definitely unaware of me. I now make it a point to follow him and at the next intersection he again happens to stop and window-shop, taking quick but normal looking glances up and down the street. I can tell that he is practiced at checking for a tail.

I decide to drop about 20 yards behind him and if I had not been watching, I might have missed him suddenly step sideways into a doorway. From my perception, one moment he was there and the next he wasn't, but I heard the click of a door shutting. I hurry to where he disappeared and come to an old doorway that looks like it hasn't been open this century. The paint is faded and chipped and the door is boarded up.

As I reach to inspect one of the strips of wood to verify that the door is sealed, I see that it's academic anyway because my hand passes through the wood. Now I know why the man can't see me; I have no substance. I decide to walk through the material of the door and pass through to the other side. I'm in a small vestibule about five feet long. In front of me is another door made of steel. I pass through it easily as well and emerge at the foot of a carpeted stairway. My Oriental friend is almost at the top. I follow.

He proceeds down a wide hallway and hesitates near a door about halfway down that opens from the inside as he approaches. A few seconds later I simply materialize through the same door.

I find myself inside a large room with a boardroom table at its center. Three men are seated at regularly spaced intervals around the table and there is room for eight or 10 more. I notice that no one sits at either head of the table. The man I followed sits down and I notice the way the men are seated there is at least two empty chairs on either side of everybody.

My man says, "Someone follows me maybe."

A man with a French accent says, "Our marshals, they sweep after you. They will stop anyone."

"Okay. I did not see them, either."

A tall man with an English accent says, "Right. We're all here. Who's going to start?"

A portly man leans forward to rest his arms on the table. Everyone notices his movement and looks toward him. "I'll get the ball rolling," he says with a mid-American accent, "Stafford. Communications. Reporting on the audio visual linkup technology. We're calling global television with sound and color a 'definite'. Out-of-atmosphere satellites are probable in 20-25 years. Routine in 30. Implications almost everywhere you look. Technologically the French and Soviets are going one way, Brits another, but we're figuring American clout'll win out.'

The heavy man sits back, obviously finished. There is not a pencil or scrap of paper anywhere on the table. The man I followed here is not the only one to be carrying nothing, there is not a briefcase in the room. Whatever is going on here is being committed to memory, and it's obviously not the first meeting of this organization, although it may be the first time these four individuals have met.

The Frenchman clears his throat to speak. "D'Altaire. Economics," he announces. "Projections are for a continuing demand for gold until a fever strikes in 25-30 years, depending on global economic recovery. After that, paper currencies will dominate, like a horserace. Incredible, but all projections are confirming."

The Englishman is staring down at the table, as if visualizing these future events with some difficulty. At last he lifts his head and says, "Smithson. Military/Political. Policy is to feed one power naturally and one artificially until the technology curve gets unsustainable. Then we pull the technology out of the false economy. Projections are 40 years, 45 outside, and the one falls. Delicate balance. Need solid data to keep it that way. We're scoring very high on government mandarin recruitment. Send all leads to Bern, please. I'm authorized to call this 'Code Yellow - Urgent'."

As the Englishman finishes his monologue he again stares down at the table surface, as if to see if his visualization is now clearer.

The man I followed now prepares to speak. His face brightens and he begins to smile, as if this is part of his delivery style. He giggles slightly, then says, "I am Lum of Human Development. After too much dark years we see hope. Our mandarins smooth the way for refugee emigration. Our restoration program is being adopted and called the Marshall Plan. Still many areas of the world are not progressing.

"I am told to say this week is 700 years since Cognoscenti first formed with an Englishman, Jew, Italian and Chinese. Since then we have been midwife to human progress. National boundaries and interests are of no concern to us. Our aim is human progress, defined as the elimination of war, pestilence and plague and to anticipate and assist the direction of human evolution.

"A dissident group formed the Contrascenti about five and a half centuries ago. That organization has since grown many cells worldwide. We will continue the struggle against them as we pursue our own aims. It should be noted this is a particularly dangerous time to conduct our affairs in an extra-governmental way, especially in America and the Soviet Union. We note with some amusement the practice of the Contras in buying into governments. Much of the wealth finds it way to us and helps our causes elsewhere while it depletes their resources. I am authorized to say we have had a good year and there are no uncontrollable issues before us for the first time in 14 years. That concludes my report."

There is silence for a moment and then the men rise to leave. I notice there are four exit doors, one at each wall. They apparently rise to leave wordlessly, but the American approaches the Chinese. Everyone stops to overhear.

"Just thought I'd mention an unlikely phenomenon, but one you might want to be aware of. Some of our members report an unseen presence, almost exclusively at executive meetings. Have you heard of such a thing?"

"I felt such a presence on my way here. We are investigating the possibility of mind travel. If that's what it is, the potential is limitless. We cannot let this fall into the Contras. It is being investigated."

Each of the men looks at the others and nods.
They depart through their designated doors.

The SubContact ends.

SubContact: Conscious Contact with our Subconscious

SubContact is achieved through a meditative state, usually with the assistance of guided imagery, which brings subconscious material to awareness. An unmistakable characteristic of SubContact is its product, a spontaneous story that invariably has a beginning, middle and end. Such stories have a metaphorical content similar to dreams and some types of purposeful meditations. The purpose in practicing SubContact is to provide, in conjunction with the personal inventory described in Chapter 2, the most efficient route to self-understanding. In the words of Socrates:

" The unexamined life is not worth living"

As you will see in the following section, SubContact is an eclectic method that borrows from four different schools of psychology. In addition, we also condense the most effective components of 12-step group support philosophy.

SubContact the program is a series of modules that have at their center the SubContact process just described. The program calls for a personal inventory of unidentified fears, knowledge of personal change, the practice of meditation and dream interpretation and techniques for 4D Thinking. In the final module, we bring SubContact to a group setting that we call GO Teams, the final chapter of this book.

What Kind of Psychology is SubContact?

There are aspects to SubContact techniques that will be familiar to Jungian psychologists. Other facets of SubContact may seem to be Freudian. Still others may be recognized as modern Cognitive-Behavioral therapy philosophy, transpersonal psychology, or they may seem to take a Gestaltist perspective. There is also an emphasis on mutual support groups and 12-step programs. We recognize these similarities and will discuss them individually. We will also explore the differences. However, in the final analysis, SubContact is a new psychology based on conscious contact with the subconscious.

SubContact and C.G. Jung

Jungians in particular will point to C. G. Jung's Active Imagination as the source of our technique. However, we developed our program in the absence of knowledge about Active Imagination, one of Jung's lesser-known practices. Some important differences in technique can be found in the delivery itself. Carl Jung advocated solo flights of the imagination, with the results later to be committed to paper or verbalized in a therapy session. We found very early in our research that the participant tends to 'forget' important details that occur in a SubContact session. This forgetting is an easy way out of dealing with material that has a tendency to be repressed, a fundamental underpinning of analytical psychology. Our research consistently points to important episodes in SubContact sessions that, if not recorded at the time of occurrence, would be lost to conscious awareness. If there is forgotten material in an unrecorded SubContact session, it cannot be examined. This compromises the purpose of the exercise by lessening the value of the material, although it may be said that when something is brought to consciousness it may come forth more readily at another time.

It was gratifying and confirming to read of Jung's Active Imagination in our third year of investigation. However, we quickly realized that the name itself contradicts the methodology of SubContact. Our process is neither 'active', which to us implies that some conscious direction takes place, nor is it 'imagination', which conjures up ideas of deliberate mental effort at imaging, like an artist conjuring up sequential cartoon panels. On this definition alone, Active Imagination describes some other procedure. A choice of words such as Passive Narration more accurately describes our technique, but we prefer the simplicity of the name SubContact.

We have enjoyed interesting discussions with neo-Jungians who protest that what Jung meant by the words Active Imagination was that the participant should be active with the material that issues forth from the imaginings in a sort of post-session analysis. This is a process we heartily endorse. We have studied Jung's work and admire, even embrace, many of his concepts. In his many volumes, we note that he is quite precise with his language. If he called his process Active Imagination, then we must conclude that he named it what he meant to name it.

In our search for knowledge, we borrow more from Jung's body of work than any other single school of thought. Frequently in the practice of SubContact, we employ such archetypal concepts as the *shadow* or unacknowledged part of ourselves. We also recognize the *animus* in women, which is the masculine representation in the psyche, as well as the female counterpart in men, the *anima*. We have no way of understanding ourselves other than as that of a *persona*, that collection of acknowledged characteristics that we hold ourselves out to be - the mask we wear and present to others. In frequent skirmishes we come to grips with a reluctant *ego*, that part of us that might be called the guardian against change, mostly by examining the root of unidentified fears. To quote Jung himself:

"Every real experience of the Self involves a defeat for the ego."

or as Krishnamurti said:

"The purpose of the ego is to resist change."

Ultimately and hopefully we strive to come to terms with *Self*. These and other concepts are borrowed gratefully from C.G. Jung. In fact, it is fair to say that *individuation*, a Jungian term, is close enough to what we mean when we say that the objective of the SubContact Program is self-understanding.

If we borrow the frequent cup of sugar from Jung, it is because he lives in the neighborhood of our type of psychology. His is the mansion on the hill.

SubContact and Sigmund Freud

There are also some apparent similarities between SubContact and Freud's 'free association', although the resemblance quickly fades upon scrutiny. Freud's technique was to have a subject reclining on a couch saying anything that came to mind and allowing that to lead to the next thought, and so on. In areas where there was resistance, Freud would claim to have identified repressed material. His treatment would then proceed based on the assumption that further examination of the repressed material would bring it to the light of day.

This assumption is quite different from having an expectation that a story will spontaneously appear, and that the metaphor contained in the story will be appropriate to the individual's present physical, mental and spiritual circumstances. One technique is in pursuit of repressed material, which is presumed to exist. SubContact, on the other hand, makes no presumptions about anything, but merely awaits an interesting subconscious yarn. If there is presumption to our process, it is that the participant will have completed their personal inventory, which would result in a reduced amount of repressed material to be available for Freudian slippage. Implicit in SubContact is the conscious willingness to welcome subconscious ... stuff.

In other words, we believe that the key first step to self-understanding is the personal inventory as described in Chapter 2. We believe that there is a direct positive correlation, that is: the more thorough the personal inventory of fears, the less fearsome is the subconscious material. To follow the inventory analogy, when a business takes inventory, it can bring to light some fairly unattractive goods. In Chapter 2 we recommend not only the personal inventory of unidentified fears as a first step, but also as a continuing practice on the way to knowing thyself. For these reasons, repressed material as such is not as important as is subconscious material brought to awareness. By our definition, the fact that something is unconscious does not necessarily mean that it is repressed.

SubContact and Cognitive-Behavioral Therapy

It is fundamental to Cognitive-Behavioral Theory that psychological problems originate with faulty thinking, which is then addressed and corrected. With SubContact, we are interested in uncovering unfounded fears, which in turn lead to unwanted behaviors such as malaloopas.

It is basic to C-B therapy that the client must come to awareness of a problem before treatment can be initiated. SubContact is similar, yet it is also different insofar as awareness is the 'treatment', if that is the right word. In comparison to the C-B meaning of awareness, the philosophy of SubContact is based on a second, or higher degree of cognizance. SubContact searches for 'why', C-B dismisses 'why' as irrelevant. With SubContact, we believe that by bringing unreasoned fear to awareness we initiate the process of eliminating the fear, and thus the unwanted behavior that originates from the fear. At the very least, our process increases behavior choices.

The SubContact philosophy of treatment agrees with the C-B position that there are no 'shoulds' and 'shouldn'ts'; these are judgmental words and phrases that have no place in our philosophy.

There are other similarities and differences between C-B theory and SubContact, but these are the essential areas of difference.

SubContact and Gestalt Therapy

The strongest similarity SubContact has with the Gestalt school is our emphasis on symbols. We have found that the examination of personal symbols that appear in SubContacts and dreams can greatly assist the individual in perspective altering. Just as in Gestalt theory, we believe that an examination of the whole and the part can be therapeutically rewarding.

SubContact and the 12 Step Program

As co-authors, we both owe a great deal to the 12 Steps of AA. That is true both personally and professionally. We believe the SubContact Program incorporates the best features of the 12-step method that has been adapted to so many different problems since the inception of AA in 1935. Specifically, the 12-step program advocates a personal inventory. We urge that our clients prepare for SubContact by first of all paving the way for change. Effective and lasting change can best be obtained by first identifying sources of fear. The 12-step program is also a spiritual program. It is our belief that self-knowledge and spirituality are inseparable.

So How Do We Do SubContact?

There are two ways to do SubContact, guided and solo. By far the best way is with a guide to help us achieve a relaxed state, to help us stay there, to prompt us if we drift too high or too low, to help us out of potentially sticky situations, to remind us of control devices and to record what we say. The following instructions apply with the assumption that a guide is present. At the end of this chapter you will find a 'Note to the Guide' as well as a sample generic guided meditation script. There are other meditations in the chapter 'Power Meditation'. If a guide is not available to you, there is a later section entitled 'Going it Alone'. In either case, please continue reading this section.

In preparation for the SubContact exercise, please read through the following material until you are familiar and comfortable with it. A few simple procedures and suggested guidelines have evolved over the years since we first began the practice of SubContact. Together with what we have mentioned in the previous modules, these suggestions will increase the likelihood of achieving and maintaining the desired level of relaxation and go a long way toward ensuring a meaningful SubContact session. The guidelines are divided into four phases: preparation, protocol, procedure and post-SubContact.

For purposes of clarity, we will be directing the following guidelines directly to the reader, using the pronoun 'you'.

SubContact Guidelines

I. Preparation

SubContact is a simple procedure. If there is a secret about it, it is in the preparation. Not only must the physical environment be favorable to SubContact, but the mental atmosphere should be conducive as well. Other than these factors, there is nothing more complicated about SubContact than preparing to have a daydream.

Let's get to the physical conditions first. The participant should be comfortable, with loose clothing and if necessary a blanket to keep warm. The temperature and room ventilation should be normal. There should be a place to completely relax. This could be a bed, sofa, floor mat, recliner, etc. Avoid sitting upright in a chair or even on the floor, this would almost certainly be distracting because of the energy required to maintain physical comfort. There should be nothing intrusive going on in the environment. Very soft background music is okay, but try to eliminate the source of harsh sounds like traffic, rock music or other distracting noises. In situations where the physical conditions are not ideal, the question becomes 'is the participant used to this level of background noise'? If the answer is yes, it may be all right to proceed; the individual may be sufficiently conditioned to the environment that it feels normal to them.

Mental preparation includes at least a nodding acquaintance with Module 1 - Change 101. The more you understand the principles behind Change 101, the more satisfying your SubContact sessions will be. At the very least, you need to be of a mind that would admit that you might have some unreasoned fears in our life. When you have reached such a conclusion you are well on our way to self-understanding.

> *"This above all: to thine own self be true..."*
> - Shakespeare

Learning to achieve a state of relaxation gets easier with time. Relax and be patient. When you realize you are experiencing a relaxed state, touch your forefinger to your thumb or use some similar cue, which you can then repeat later to make it easier to achieve this state again.

Have someone read a guided meditation to you. You will find a sample meditation at the end of this chapter. The voice of the guide should be pleasant sounding to you as well as calm, even and unhurried.

Ensure that your guide is prepared and equipped to write down everything you say. Alternatively, you may want to have the session tape-recorded. Keep in mind that it is very helpful to have a verbatim record at the conclusion of your session. After all, this is your subconscious material and the objective is to come to understand the meaning of it. Use low lighting, or use an eye cover if you are doing the exercise during the day. Bright light hinders mental imagery for most people.

If you are out of sorts, overly tired, emotionally upset, have consumed alcohol, or if you are using mind-altering drugs, postpone this activity until you are more stable.

2. Protocol

Obtaining an appropriate level of relaxation and experiencing mental imagery are fairly easy things to do. However,

to achieve the state of SubContact it is necessary for you to *trust*. You must trust your guide, trust that the process will occur and trust yourself. In this connection, there are a few points to keep in mind:
- Remember that your subconscious is part of you and it will give you only what you can handle, when you can handle it.
- Remember that you are in control at all times, and you allow only what you want to come into your SubContact.
- Remember that you are protected while in SubContact. Symbolically, a pure white light can represent this protection.
- Remember that you can arm yourself with some universal device, such as a phaser, that you can use for any number of things. For example, it can be a light, a communication tool, it can transport you to another place. Take a magic tool with you.
- Expect experts and specialists to be available to you. If they don't start showing up fairly quickly, invent them exactly as you'd like them to be. After that, it is important to trust them to have the abilities you're looking for. Let them be themselves - you must not be actively directing things in SubContact.
- Remember that you can open your eyes at any time to end your session.
- Remember that shadow or negative aspect material may appear. This is no cause for alarm because you control events, even if it is just to open your eyes. You will frequently be *invited* to explore shadow material, but if you care not to, simply turn in a different direction, normally, but not always, to your right.
- Remember to believe everything you see, hear and feel, because at this particular moment in time and space it is true.

"Dreams are real while they are happening. Can we say anymore about life?" - Havelock Ellis

The shadow side, or negative aspect is always with you and will present itself in some form, such as a dark, left-opening doorway, or an unappealing figure of a person or animal. Sometimes a clownish person can represent the Shadow, although you will sense insincerity in their words or antics. At this point, simply ignore it and chose to go in another direction, or tell whatever it is to go away. Or you can blast it with your phaser. Or you can simply open your eyes. The choices are yours to make and they are unlimited; you have control at all times. You are advised to explore the shadow side after you are more experienced with the SubContact process.

3. Procedure

It is important that you know what to expect and expect what to know. This section on Procedure and the next one on Post-SubContact will tell you with both. This section will prepare you to know what to expect.

Especially in the early part of the session, follow the words of your guide as much as possible. Once something begins to occur, let your guide know by starting to talk about what you see, hear, feel, smell, intuit, etc. At a time like this, don't be concerned about manners; just start talking. You will learn to speak without affecting your state of relaxation; almost anyone can talk from this state.

There is invariably a right time to begin relating your experiences. It's very much like riding a bike; it looks difficult, but once you've got the hang of it, it's very easy. So be prepared to start talking, either when the guide asks you to, or earlier if you sense something significant is being presented in your mind's eye. You will be surprised at how easy it is to narrate what you experience in a session.

Have the expectation that you will experience some degree of mental imaging. Expect it to get clearer and more complex as you become more familiar with the process. Like any activity, you can only get better with practice. Remember that mental imaging is the process of using all of your senses. At first you may be stronger in one modality than another. For example, you may see better than you hear, or vice versa. As you gain experience with SubContact, you will find that you can increase the efficiency of every one of your senses. Learn to adjust quality of image, sharpen the focus, increase audio volume, etc. Keep in mind that everyone dreams, so you already know how to do mental imaging.

Continue talking to your guide until you feel that the session is over. In our experience spanning over ten years, SubContact sessions have always ended when they were supposed to. SubContact has a life of its own.

Be patient and go with the flow as long as it feels comfortable to do so. A little discomfort is okay; a situation that arouses fear may be a suggestion to go elsewhere, but that's up to you. Expect that control is in your hands, don't settle for anything less. As you need them, develop your own personal tools, for example why walk when you can fly? Why climb mountains when you can create escalators? If you want to meet with someone, just reach for your phaser and put in a call, etc.

People appear in SubContact. Sometimes it's one person, sometimes two or three and sometimes a host of people show up. When someone shows up, begin to interact. Ask who they are, what their names are, what they represent. Trust your instincts about when to talk and when to listen. It is probably very wise to do a lot more listening than talking. Be sure to describe the age, appearance, sex, etc. of the people you see - this information can be handy later.

Try to have a little more courage in SubContact than you do in real life. It's an amazing byproduct, but for example, if you have trouble with public speaking and you are in a SubContact populated by an arena full of people - start talking!

Your subconscious mind cannot distinguish between reality and fantasy, and if you are experiencing yourself as a public speaker, you will feel more and more comfortable in that role in real life.

It is helpful to enter a SubContact session prepared. For example, take a problem or a question along with you. You will find that 'why' questions are the best. It is unpredictable, but sometimes you'll be rewarded with new information or perhaps a different perspective. It is not essential to do this, and sometimes your direct concerns will not be addressed anyway, but it is best to be prepared.

Many people experience SubContact as having a starting point, such as beginning with a symbol, or representation, or a particular scene of some kind, then proceed with a feeling of exploring or going somewhere on an adventure. This feeling of movement may occur several times during the session. Go with it. Movement may be represented as going up or down an elevator, travelling through a tunnel, flying over scenes, or riding in a vehicle. When the SubContact experience is coming to a close, the participant will often end up back at the same or a similar starting point.

Whatever you see, hear and feel, be sure and relate it to your recording guide, just as you experience it. Include any intuition, or insight, that comes to you. *Do Not Edit!* If you alter or amend what you experience, you change the record of what your subconscious had to say. That would be a literal case of fooling yourself and would render the session pointless.

Expect one of four main types of SubContact:

- **Normal:** This would describe 90+% of all SubContact sessions. A SubContact session may be considered normal if it contains a minimal amount of any or all of the other types. No one of the other three types will have dominated the theme of the SubContact.

- **Creative:** In this type of session, a problem or question may be addressed in a systematic way. Perhaps you've had a question in the back of your mind, or this may be the result of deliberately bringing a problem to SubContact for solution. Enjoy!

- **Dark Side:** Generally you will know when you're dealing with Shadow material, although the content may be so mild that you are unsure. If you have any doubt at all, evaluate the material as if it came from your Shadow side. Shadow material does not mean only violent or mucky stuff. It may be experienced as an evil leer or vague emotional unease. We urge you not to be too concerned about Shadow material; it's around. Always keep in mind that you make all decisions about continuing in any direction. However, if you ever sense the presence of *evil*, open your eyes. Evil is the darkest of the dark side and you will know its presence. Evil cannot be outthought, so open your eyes.

- **Libido**: marked by a sexual theme, usually part of one of the other types. We've never heard of a purely sexual SubContact, but when opposite sexes are together in SubContact there may be sexual energy or charged situations. At times, for example, a man and woman may suddenly appear who look somewhat disheveled: hair out of place, clothes in disarray, etc. A reasonable person may conclude that they have just finished making love. This is interesting only insofar as who or what the people represent to you and what a sexual union of these two representations might mean to you.

4. **Post-SubContact:**

Now you now know what to expect. Following such an experience you should also expect what to know. That is what this section is all about.

You may have just returned from the most exciting journey of your life, or perhaps you experienced a merely peaceful, insightful SubContact. No matter what your experiences were, there are now recommended procedures to follow. Keep it foremost in your mind that you've just received a message from your subconscious. Although we may be tempted to just let it be, we need to get into the habit of deciphering the message from our subconscious. It is *here*, in our recorded SubContact session, that the payoff exists.

Here is the procedure to follow:
- Ask your guide to read the transcript back to you. You may recall details that you missed commenting on in the rush of events of SubContact. Now is the time to bring the record up to date.
- Summarize the overall experience. Was it positive and uplifting? Was it a downer? Or was it just interesting? Write down the emotional tone of your session.
- Take some time and read through the transcript, decoding and interpreting the session as you learned to do in Module 3: Dream Language. Examine the language, symbols, metaphors and context.
- Remember that there are always at least two meanings, so if you've only found one, keep digging; there's gold there.
- SubContact always has something positive in it for you, find it and bring it into your waking life.
- Honor yourself and honor the process of SubContact by reflecting on how you can best use what you have learned.
- Some SubContact sessions may be represented as a metaphorical story. Others seem disjointed, but may have a recurring theme running through the different scenarios. Look for these and make a note of them.
- Come back to your transcript at a later time, and look for additional meanings and insights into your

life. Review the appropriateness of the SubContact session from the point of view of 20/20 hindsight.

Note for the Guide

It may be difficult for you to write down everything your partner says, so leave out unnecessary words, such as 'a', 'the', etc. You might want to use a version of speedwriting, where you can shorten words without losing their meaning (mean^g).

Remember that you are there as an interactive guide as well as a recordist. Be alert for occasions when the silence is prolonged, when you need to make a mild interjection, a gentle reminder to continue talking. At such times, quietly ask, *'and what do you sense now?'* or *'what is happening?'* That is often enough. It is important to be unobtrusive, yet to also be there for your partner.

A Sample Meditation Script for a SubContact Session

Read or record the following meditation at a moderate to slow pace. It is like a recipe for good soup, you can change it to suit your taste. After a period of time, the participant doing SubContact will find that the process is a self-evolving one. That is, after the guide gives the initial relaxing suggestions, your subconscious will provide the stimuli to reach the desired level of relaxation. Ask your guide to emphasize what works for you in your next SubContact session. By the same token, eliminate any part of the script you find distracting. Communicate with your guide. Then relax, and enjoy the journey.

Sample Meditation

    Take a moment and allow yourself to be comfortable . . . be aware of your body, ... know that your entire body is secure and well supported. . . when you breathe in, breathe in relaxation, . . . to every part of your body. When you breathe out, breathe out any tension you feel in your body. . . Breathe in relaxation, . . and when you breathe out, let go of any tension, worries or fears you might have.
    As you breathe in feel a refreshing breath bringing nurturing energy of healing, protection and blessing to your body, .. to every cell of your body.
    As you breathe out, imagine that the tension becomes a part of a cycle, an ongoing cycle of transformation . . . like the rain drops that fall from the clouds and form little rivulets that run into streams, and then into bigger rivers that flow to the ocean.
    And perhaps, with the next breath, you can imagine . . . deep inside of yourself, a feeling of calm and relaxation. And as you put your awareness on that feeling, begin to imagine that this feeling is like a musical instrument. And it makes a sound. And listen to the sound of that feeling. And as you hear that sound of calm and relaxation, perhaps . . . you can make the feeling stronger, and the sense of calm . . . and relaxation can begin to move, gently, like a slow, gentle wave, to every part of your body.
    And as you hear that sound and feel that feeling, perhaps, as you take your next breath, you can see the color of that sound, of that feeling, of calm and relaxation, as it moves gently through all of your body. And as you sense that color of calm and relaxation, perhaps, as you take your next breath you can smell that color, . . . you can smell that sense of relaxation and notice what it smells like to you deep inside of you. And notice what that smell might taste like? So that you can smell and taste that color, that sound, that sense, of calm and relaxation.

And perhaps, with the next breath you will allow a screen to be pulled across your mind's eye, . . . and when you are ready, allow images to freely flow across your screen. And perhaps you can take a moment now to adjust your screen, . . . use your controls, you have them with you. Perhaps you need to make the screen brighter, or bigger, the images sharper, clearer. Just take a moment to allow the images to flow across your screen.

And when you are ready, you may . . . begin to describe what is happening.

Going it Alone

If a guide is not available to you there are certain procedures you can follow to obtain the benefits of SubContact. You will require a system for achieving a meditative state and a method of recording your SubContact session.

Probably the best way to arrive at an appropriate mental state is by listening to a tape or CD made for that purpose. There are many excellent meditative recordings on the market, including our own. You can obtain details on our CD by going to **subcontact.com**, and clicking the Power Meditation icon. There is, of course, a shortcoming to having an inanimate guide, not the least of which is the ability to shut it off without disturbing yourself when you have achieved the desired state. A remote control can be very handy for this purpose, but be careful to memorize the position of the *off* or *mute* button so you can trigger it effortlessly. Otherwise, keep the volume at the absolute minimal level so that you can get the gist of what is being said and/or the background music, without impairing the quality of your SubContact.

There are two ways to record what you see, hear and feel in SubContact. One way is to write it down right after its conclusion. The shortcoming here, as we've pointed out earlier, is that you may 'forget' certain key elements of the session. There is an almost exquisite dilemma here because *what* you would tend to forget is exactly what you need to examine. In this context, the process of *forgetting,* in psychoanalytic theory, is a selective one and betrays hidden conflict.

The best way to chronicle your journey is by audiotape. Right off the bat this may present you with some problems, such as having an audio CD to listen to and control and another to record on. However, an accurate record of your journey is worth the possible awkwardness.

Note:
We've been blessed with ideal conditions from the start of our research. As a result, we have limited experience and advice for those who have to go it alone. If you are in this position, and have found a tip or technique that works for you, please let us know. We'd love to hear from you. We can be contacted at info @subcontact.com.

Chapter 7

Module 6 - GO Teams

From the Journals of SubContact: **Growing Water**

 I am travelling through space at what must be the speed of light. As I pass stars and planets I feel the slight tug of gravity from each body and know they affect my course. I am approaching a planet that looks barren, like a desert; there are no seas or trees.

 I am suddenly on the ground and now I'm easily rising up a rock face, high on a mountain, and approach a huge circular skyscraper built on sturdy columns that rise out of what appears to be a dry riverbed. It is dusk but I can see that the building is a rich blue color and lights blaze from the complex, showing the barren landscape outside.

 I want to be inside the building and suddenly I am. A man is waiting for me. He wears a white smock like a scientist and has a clipboard tucked under his arm. We approach each other.

 He extends his hand in greeting and says, "I wasn't sure where you'd be coming from, so I waited here."

 I know that he knows I am from Earth, so I take his meaning to be that he did not know where in the building I would appear.

 "Let me show you our facility," he says, and there is uncommon pride in his voice and manner. He leads me to a door and when he opens it he steps aside and allows me to pass.

 I am standing at a balcony high up, maybe fifty stories above the ground floor. The balcony runs around the outer wall facing a colossal curving inner core that is the heart of the building. The structure is a huge skyscraper that projects at least another 50 stories upward and is topped by a dome. As I approach the railing, I feel a little dizzy looking far *down to the ground level where ant-sized people move about with a purpose. The scale of the operation is mind-boggling.*

"What do you do here? I mean, what is the purpose of this building?"

He smiles and says, "We grow water."

"Grow water? I've never heard of such a thing. How do you accomplish that?" I ask him.

"With people. People who love to do what they do. Come with me, let me show you."

I follow him around the balcony and he comes to a door. He pushes a button on the wall and what appears to be elevator doors slide open and we enter. I cannot see which button he pushes and cannot tell whether we're traveling up or down until the door opens again. We step out at the ground level that I looked down upon earlier.

People are going about their work in a dedicated manner. What is notable is that everyone seems to be happy. I can tell that their smiles are genuine.

My guide leads me to a young woman who is conducting her work beside a bowl-shaped structure with a large pile of large rocks in the middle. The vessel is about ten feet across and at waist level. The bowl is nearly full of very crisp blue water. The water is bubbling and I get the feeling it is dancing joyously.

She becomes aware of us for the first time and smiles, as she says enthusiastically, "Isn't this wonderfully clear and happy water? This is my second crop today."

I don't know what to say to her and notice they are both looking at me as if they're waiting for me to comprehend something. Finally, to avoid silence, I say, "It looks like water. It looks very clear."

My guide smiles and nods to the young woman as he leads me in the direction of a middle-aged man. As we walk along he says to me, "All the people here are chosen because they love their work. Everybody here has a 'wet thumb'."

This sounds very strange to me and I stop in the hope that he will elaborate. My guide keeps going and stands beside the man we were approaching. I join them.

The middle-aged man is working beside a bowl structure identical to the last one and is as pre-occupied with his work as the young woman was. The water in his container also seems to contain a spirit of its own, as if nurturing has added some additional happy quality to the liquid. After a moment the man turns to us.

"This is my finest crop ever," he says proudly. "I believe its purity is one-half drop short of perfection. Observe the clarity and notice the hint of blue, which is the hallmark of purity." It was delicious looking water and looked as effervescent as the previous batch we'd seen.

Since my guide seems to expect me to clue in by myself, which I don't, I decide to ask the operator.

"What are you growing here? Surely you make or grow something ... else?"

He looks astonished, as if I have splashed him with cold water. He looks at my guide who smiles and nods assent. "We grow water," the man says.

I don't understand and can just repeat his words, "You grow water. Nothing else, you just grow water?"

My guide says to the man, "Do you have a show pan?"

"Yes Why? Are you going to tickle the devil's snout?"

My guide nods and the worker produces a metal pan shaped like a tray with a slight concave depression in it. The worker walks to the other side of his workstation and dips the pan carefully into the far edge of the water, as if he is removing a weed. He sifts through the pan and flicks some of the water back into the pool as if selecting wheat from chaff, mineral from ore. I can guess that the happiest water ends up back in the pool.

He carefully hands the pan to my guide and says, "Can I watch? It always inspires me."

My guide nods assent.

Gesturing toward me, the worker asks my guide, "Does he know about The Evil Force?"

My guide accepts the pan from the man and I notice the bottom is barely covered by water. He says to me, "There is a negative energy on this planet that is full of hatred. It imposes its will on the planet by destroying every particle of water. These facilities, and hundreds of others like it on this planet, were specially built to grow water. The Evil Force cannot gain entry to the buildings. We have a plan that is nearing completion. But first let me demonstrate the Force."

He leads me to what looks like a rectangular glass window in the wall. I can see that it is about two feet deep and that there is another door on the other side, through which I can see a starry night.

He pushes a button and the glass window slides up. He places the tray of water inside and activates the button again and it closes with a hiss. My guide and the workman step closer and I notice other workers have gathered around as well.

My guide hesitates and looks around, as if waiting for last minute stragglers, then apparently satisfied, he pushes another button and the outside window slides up.

Almost immediately there is a silent rage of activity within the pan. Drops of water become tracer bullets that shoot out violently as if from an unseen attack. Brightly colored sparks fly in every direction and I cannot tell for sure whether the bullet-like streaks are action, reaction, or both. I feel that something is slaking its thirst for hatred.

Within seconds the violent fireworks are over. There is silence in the room. My guide activates the button that slides the outside door closed and when it clicks shut he opens the inside door. He slowly withdraws the now dry tray and there is silence in the room. This lasts only for a moment, then the workers return to their labor of love with renewed motivation.

My guide tells me that the time to engage the Evil Force is near. As he describes the plan to me I see it unfold. At a *precisely timed moment this facility and hundreds of other plants all over the planet will release huge amounts of nurtured water. In the ensuing maelstrom, The Force will be so divided by the onslaught of life-giving water that it will be washed away in a sea of its own hatred.*

I see it all happening. I feel the rage of The Force as it divides itself again and again and again until it cannot divide itself against another drop of liquid. The dry riverbeds are suddenly quenched with rushing water. I see that in time clouds form and the cycle of life-giving liquid is sustained. I see plants and animals begin to multiply.

The people who love their work move on to other places where their love for what they do in life is needed. There is always somewhere in the universe that could use some loving care.

The SubContact ends.

GO Teams

A Brief History

GO Teams is the final module of the SubContact program. GO Teams is that point where we take our search for self-discovery to a mutual support group setting. The natural time to consider forming or joining a GO Team is when we have a goal.

Mutual support groups (MSGs) are the most effective method ever created for overcoming obstacles. The effectiveness of MSGs is evident in its ever-growing popularity. There is a MSG for almost any purpose. We believe the time has come to extend the benefits of a MSG to the quest for a personal goal.

Much of Bob's doctoral thesis research centered on the proliferation of MSGs. For example, sociologists Room and Greenfield found in a survey that almost 15% of the adult population of the U.S. have attended some form of 12-step meeting. That is an astonishing number of people to be familiar with MSG therapy. It should be noted that we use the terms mutual support group and 12-step meetings almost interchangeably, although AA and its addiction oriented offshoots have as their purpose the alleviation of negative behavior. In conceiving of GO Teams, we have in mind the benefits of mutual assistance, so that our objective makes no assumptions of an existing problem, but rather anticipates positive achievement.

"GO Teams is for what you want to do, not what you want to stop doing." - **Dian Benson**

The still growing phenomenon of MSG exists today because of a historic meeting of two men in Akron, Ohio in 1935. These two men, Bill W. and Dr. Bob, discovered that by helping one another reach a common goal they were helping themselves as well. That's how AA was born. Sometimes what we can't do alone, we can do together. It is from this basic idea that groups, from the earliest to the latest, have as their guiding principle. Based on the same idea, GO Teams is a mutual support group for achieving personal goals.

What we mean by personal goals can encompass almost anything, and will almost invariably possess an element that leads to self-fulfillment. Another thing it would almost certainly be is something we have never been able to accomplish on our own. With the support of others, who are concerned and committed to seeing us achieve that goal, we increase our chances of a successful outcome. Is it also possible that helping others to achieve their goals would help us to achieve our own objectives? That's been our experience. It is a rare goal that is achieved in a vacuum; we almost always need the help of others if the objective is worthwhile. When we reflect on our past achievements, we realize they were more easily achieved when we received some encouragement from family and friend.

The Dynamics of Mutual Support Groups (MSG)

One of the most important factors in the success of any mutual support group is the individual member's belief that the supportive nature inherent to the group makes a difference. Our individual need for support contributes to the group's existence. The support given to the participants by way of encouragement and social acceptance can have as much positive effect on the individual as the stated purpose can. The group purpose is the primary motivating factor that attracts and keeps each member. The group purpose includes the methods, ideas and suggested guidelines for fulfilling that objective. Guidelines are important to ensure that each of the participants agrees to support the group as a whole for mutual benefit.

GO Teams have as their common purpose a commitment to help each member reach their personal goal. Each member in turn agrees to learn and practice the SubContact Modules in order to help each other, and themselves, to achieve their objective. This member commitment to fulfill their obligation is a contributing factor to the success of support groups. One other ingredient that goes toward creating a healthy support group is success itself. When we can achieve any measure of success, we generate energy that can be felt and shared by each member. We feel good about ourselves and it shows. Our GO Teams supporters are motivated as much by our own achievements as the encouragement we have been willing to give them to reach their goals.

"We can do what I can't do." - Anonymous

Conversely, if a group fails to meet the needs of the participants in one way or another, it ceases to exist.

Support groups can be formed for just about anything two or more people want to achieve. All groups meet certain criteria or they will not endure. The group will survive only as long as the majority of the members agree to adhere to the guidelines that are consistent with its purpose. These guidelines, otherwise known as the group norms, may be explicit, such as in a written code of behavior, or implicit, behavior that is expected but not always stated. A group may dissolve after achieving its goal, or become an ongoing entity that adapts to the changing needs of the membership.

We, the authors, developed and wrote the material for this book, and our thanks go out to every person who contributed to its completion. For instance, we could not have developed the SubContact program without the first group, with whom we originally shared our ideas and tried out our budding techniques in Calgary many years ago. It was the GO Team members in Victoria, BC that asked the questions that helped us articulate and refine our material for this book. Without them, there could be no program, no techniques and no book.

Why the Name GO Teams?

G.O. stands for Goal Oriented. The name GO Teams is the result of a 4D Thinking session and a meditation that took place one afternoon in Brisbane, Australia. It was the first time we put all of our concepts for personal achievement under one name. Up until then we had been sharing various aspects of our work in each of the SubContact modules, but it was not yet a unit.

We learned that together we were able to accomplish more than we had been able to do on our own. As the saying goes, two heads are better than one. We recognized GO Teams as the medium for delivering our modular program and the opportunity to practice techniques.

Our experiences with goal-oriented activities taught us that personal understanding was both a result of and a prerequisite to setting and reaching our goals. A specific project is an excellent opportunity for exploring material from our subconscious.

"We get by with a little help from our friends."
- The Beatles

Checklist for Forming GO Teams

If you would like to form a GO Team, here is a checklist of things to do that we have found useful.

1. Commit to become part of a shared resource group:
   - share with GO Teams members your knowledge and expertise to facilitate their goal achievement.
   - participate at group meetings to the best of your ability.
   - share an appropriate amount of time outside meetings to help in goal achievement, e.g. e-mail, telephone, etc.
   - share other resources, such as professional services, only as each member chooses to do so.

1. Set and achieve a goal that meets the following criteria:
   - every goal needs to be achievable, that is, it needs to be within the capabilities of the member.
   - every goal needs to be morally and ethically deserving of other members' support.
   - every member's goal is therefore worthy of support.
   - every goal needs to contain a number of steps or shorter term goals.
   - short term goals on the way to longer term goals will serve as interim goals. All long-term goals have shorter-term objectives that must be achieved first.
   - every goal needs to be set within a timeframe, allowing for reasonable adjustments.
   - every goal has a satisfactory conclusion.

2. Continue to practice the Modules of SubContact, e.g. 4D Thinking, SubContact, etc., to help you and each member

achieve a particular goal. A large group may need to divide into smaller groups for this purpose.

3. Within the group meeting, allow each member time to share on the status of their goal.

4. Encourage group members to attend/create other events with other group members.

5. The group has the option to suggest change, or disagree with any of the above.

Join a GO Teams Online

If you want information on how to form a GO Team locally, go to our website, www. subcontact.com and look for the e-Bureau icon.

> *"Forget the past. No one becomes successful in the past."* - Josh Billings

SubContact of Others

All of the SubContact sessions you have read so far have been ours. The reason for this is that we can simply delve into the accumulating Journals of SubContact to retrieve a session with an appropriate theme. These Journals now span more than a decade.

For a change, and to demonstrate the remarkable similarities people experience in SubContact, we offer an example of a SubContact session from one of our GO Teams participants. 'S' is female, middle aged, and was first attracted to our seminars out of curiosity about unidentified fears. After attending a few sessions of GO Teams, she volunteered to participant in three SubContact sessions with Dian as her guide. The following is an unedited transcription of her third session. One evening she read it to some of her colleagues.

From a SubContact Session of "S"

It seems we're in a place like Warsaw. The buildings are kind of gray. The people moving around, like Jewish people, I see the Star of David on their shoulders, are in a ghetto. Everything is quite gray; the streets are empty with the occasional motorcar parked on the side of the street. And there are people there, but it is difficult to pick out which people need to be focused on. I sense young children are there.

A couple of young girls are coming down the street. They have schoolbooks with them, but they are afraid to be happy, to smile, because something bad will happen to them if they do. They have pigtails and tartan skirts and knee-highs on. They go into a building and clatter up the stairs. They look around, afraid their clatter will cause trouble too. And when you look at their clothes, you can see that they are clean and cared for, but threadbare. At the top of the stairs they come into a suite, their mother's there. There is laundry hanging on racks in the apartment. Everything is shabby, but again well scrubbed, well tended; and the girls know there is love in that apartment. They go and embrace their mother and then go into the bedroom.

Their grandmother is there in bed. She has the most beautiful face, a mother superior; the beauty is shining through her eyes. The girls each go to a side of the bed. There is a crucifix above the head of the bed. Each girl takes one of their grandmother's hands and tells her about their day. As they are doing this there is a pounding on the door. They hear their mother gasp, but they've learned not to rush places. Quietly, they go to the door of the bedroom. They can see soldiers at the door; they have helmets on, like beetle shells, and they have ugly mean faces. The soldiers grab their mother, who turns to them even though the soldiers don't know the girls are there, she pleads with them, her eyes tell them not to say anything.

The mother wants to fight the soldiers, but she knows she doesn't dare in order to protect her children. The soldiers slam out the door, dragging her with them. She is weeping as she goes down the stairs, because she knows she may never see her family again.

The girls go to the door and peep out; they know they have to look after their grandmother now. They want to find their father, to tell him what happened. The girls are strangely calm, they know they have to be strong to survive. They go back to the bedroom to make sure their grandmother is resting comfortably. The girls give her a cup of tea, and they don't tell her what has happened. They tell her that mama has gone to the store, and they have to go find papa and tell him it's time for dinner.

So they go, and this time they don't clatter down the stairs; they walk very carefully, silently, and they don't go openly down the street. They walk along close to the buildings, watching, making sure everything is safe. They see neighbors, people they know, but they don't tell them their troubles. They feel it will just bring more trouble to other people. They find their father working in a printing factory.

There is a lot of machinery, people scurrying here and there, the light is sort of greenish inside the building. They go to their papa and they start to tremble then, and shake, because it's finally beginning to hit them, what has happened. They tell him what's gone on, and he turns pale like he is going to faint. His best friend comes over, and he tells his friend that the Gestapo has taken his wife.

His best friend says, "What are we going to do to get her back?"

"First of all, we need to find out where they have taken her."

The friend says, "There are many children in this place, and they've learned to be very quiet, but they see a lot. We'll send the children; they can crawl through the tunnels where others don't go."

He calls some children from the back room, two or three little boys, very skinny with big dark eyes that stand out in their faces. He tells them to find the mother and they scamper off.

Their noses are runny; they are very quick, agile and inventive. They do find out where the mother is, they can see her. Her legs are tied together at the ankles, her hands are tied behind the chair, and that evil man is yelling right in her face.

"Tell us what we want to know, Jewess."

She whimpers and moans, but she's not telling them anything.

They're saying to her, "We know you are hiding people, hiding money, hiding information. Important information we need." They hit her then, hard, and her head just flops, but she doesn't talk.

One of them says, "Forget it, she's useless to us; we'll send her on the train tomorrow. And if we can roundup those scummy family of hers, they're going too."

The boys scamper back down their little hidey-holes, their tunnels, back to Papa and his best friend, and they tell him.

Papa says, "Oh my God, I was afraid it would come to this; my poor Elsa, my poor, poor Elsa."

He knows he has to leave his wife where she is, he must try to save his girls, his mother, himself, so his girls will have him. He can't think now about his grief, he'll have to think later about his grief.

The girls, the father, are outside now, by a train station. They have one little suitcase. The train's coming, it stops and they get on. The grandmother has been left with neighbors. When they get in the train, it is filled with people that all look the same as them, haunted, pale and worried. There are all these little family groupings, some have a father, some a mother, but all are missing at least one important family member.

The conductor comes in and he says this train will take all of them to safety; it's the Glory Train. So they try to calm their fears and hope they have made the right choices. The *train starts off. It is very hot and smelly, even though people try to be as clean as they can, but it's very hard when there are no washing facilities. The people still try to be respectful; they're joined in their suffering.*

The train goes through the night and every once in awhile you can hear the train's whistle; it's almost like a moan. They go through a long dark tunnel inside a mountain. A very long tunnel, it seems like it's going on forever. It seems as if they need to go through that long tunnel, and they need to bear with it, that it's so long and so dark.

The train breaks through the other end of the tunnel. There is a beautiful forest on the other side and the grayness is going; there is more color in the grass and the trees. The trees are like poplars, the wind is rustling in the leaves, sunlight is beginning to fill the cars and the people are a little less fearful. They are still fearful.

The train moves along and soon comes into a station; this station is safe. When they get off the train, all their missing relatives are there, and they feel like it's a joke, a big cosmic joke almost. They just have to touch them and feel their clothing to make sure they are real, to believe it.

"How can this be? How can you be here?"

"We seem to be chosen; it seems we've been chosen. We are so blessed. We must all be together now, we must be strong, we must be united. There's another place for us, not here, another place, our own. It won't be easy for us, but that's where we have to go, that's where we belong."

The girls' mother was there; she was one of the group and she said, "I was in the cell and then I was here. It's a miracle; it really is a miracle."

Everybody, all the families together, got down on their knees and thanked God for bringing them here, bringing them together, for showing them what their next step was on their journey.

That's the end.

That's the end of this story perhaps, but for S it is probably also the beginning of the process of self-discovery. As she finished reading the transcript and placed the transcript on her knee, she looked off into space as she said, "The only thing I can't figure out is what the crucifix was doing over the grandmother's bed."

During the reading, one of S's colleagues, 'B', had been listening with growing incredulity.

"That's exactly what it was like," 'B' said quietly. "I was there. My mother and grandmother were Catholic, my father was Jewish. That's why there was a crucifix."

'B', who was 75, had spent her childhood years during WWII in Hitler's Austria. 'S' was completely unaware of 'B's personal history.

We don't try to make anything more out of this than what it was: an unlikely coincidence. However, when we examine some of Jung's constructs, such as the Collective Unconscious, even we sometimes wonder.

"Coincidence is God's work when sHe chooses to remain anonymous" - Anonymous

A Final Word on Obsession

Once you have defined a goal as worthwhile to you, **get obsessed about it!** This does not mean let the rest of your life go to pot, for we always urge balance in our lives. What it does mean is that we can safely set aside a part of our lives that is devoted to our own *magnificent obsession.* So get *compulsed* about your goal!

Chapter 8

The End of the Beginning

From the Journals of SubContact: **The Revolutionist**

I was a lowly officer in the French Revolutionary army. My orders were to arrest - and hang - a woman in a village who was known to be a Royalist. But a priest stood in my way, literally and figuratively. The clergyman was of small stature but of great heart, and although he knew where the woman was hiding in the village, no amount of threats could pry the information from him.

I decided to announce my intention to hang him in the hope that word would reach the ears of the woman I sought and she would surrender herself before the cleric was dispatched. A rope was strung over a tree, a noose was snugged around the priest's neck and my sergeant offered his horse to complete the gallows. The life of the priest was held in suspense somewhere between my reluctant order and a skittish horse, upon which he sat, trussed up. He appeared to be prepared to meet his maker.

It was at this moment that a beautiful woman entered the Town Square. She carried herself with regal bearing that belied the peasant clothes she wore. At the sight of her, I was in conflict with myself; for on the one hand I could now free the priest but on the other hand I must execute this distinguished and beautiful woman.

Many thoughts went through my mind, including the question of the loyalty of my ragtag company of troops, some of whom were grumbling darkly at the prospect of being party to this execution.

The burly sergeant muttered, "A New France, yes. But a New France with honor!"

I turned to a corporal and another soldier standing beside him and pointed to the sergeant. "Seize him!" I ordered "Disarm him and tie his hands."

Gesturing toward the priest, I then commanded, "Free this man."

The priest had been looking down on these events from astride the sergeant's horse with serene indifference. A couple of my troops helped him dismount and unbound his hands.

I beckoned the woman to come to me, which she did with dignity. We stood looking at each other while those around us were engaged in great activity.

The corporal was soon at my elbow. "What do you want done with the sergeant?" he asked with some trepidation.

"Put him astride the horse."

"And me, sir," the woman said with a cultured accent, "what will you have done with me?"

"My orders are to execute anyone who stands in the way of the Republic. That means any priest, any sergeant or any woman."

The priest had joined her side. He watched me, not with fear, but with fascination.

The woman said, "You did not answer my question, Captain. What will you have done with me?"

I gazed at her for some time. Thoughts of ultimate power played in my head. What had put me in this position except my own set of political beliefs? What kind of basis were political beliefs for taking a life? The conflict within me raged.

Finally I responded to the woman, "What will I have done with you? I will have you go across the street to the sanctuary of the church. Seek a place there to meditate, and when you have concluded that we now live in a New France, a republic of the people, you may then leave."

Perhaps it was her courageous bearing that did not falter, perhaps it was the slump of her shoulders at hearing my pardon, but somehow I knew she would no longer resist the revolution.

I was finished here, except for one thing. With the back of my hand I swatted the sergeant's horse. With him aboard,

hands still tied, the horse skittered off with the sergeant teetering precariously in the saddle.
This new order called for new ways of doing things.

The SubContact ends.

Something Happened

More than a decade ago, something happened. Yes, Bob had met his wife Dian by that time, but there was something else. Yes, we had both been free of alcohol for some time by then - but it was something more than that too. For one day Dian said, "Let me take you on a guided meditation."

We were familiar with meditating prior to this, and tried to practice it, but with modest result. However, when Bob ventured forth under Dian's guidance, something happened.

Perhaps it was the flawless and calm delivery. Perhaps it was the soothing quality of her voice. Perhaps it was the compelling imagery that she began to paint in front of his mind's eye. Perhaps it was the combination of all of these, but the point is, something happened.

On that first meditation we went to France. Not to Paris in the modern day, but to a modest village that was being torn by the forces of the French Revolution. And so began what has been a most remarkable experience. Bob cannot vouch for the historical accuracy of the French Revolution because he doesn't know much about it. He hasn't any idea whether the Revolutionaries went about the countryside executing Royalists. Bob is ignorant of French history.

At the time we were amazed at the detail he saw in the meditation. The experience was as authentic as if he had been there with the real emotion of real people, including his own emotional investment.

In the time that followed, we were quite sure there was a logical explanation for such an occurrence. One characteristic of the meditation, one that we could not overlook, was that there were parallels between his story of the French captain and our own lives. For we, too, found that there was a new order in our lives, one that called for a new way of doing things.

Then we experienced another guided meditation. The setting for this one was hundreds of years and thousands of miles from the first one. Although it was different, it had the same sense of realism and the same uncanny detail. There were two other similarities: we lived another story, one with a beginning, middle and ending. The story was once again metaphorical; it also applied to an aspect of our lives that needed attention.

Today, as psychologists looking back on these events of several years ago, it seems to us now that we were slow in twigging to the pattern that was emerging. When we did realize something was going on, it was with the knowledge that there were several factors of equal importance:
- the meditations required guidance.
- there was always a spontaneous story with a beginning, middle and ending.
- the story was always metaphorical.
- the metaphor was always applicable to one or both of our lives.

Understanding the significance of these factors kept us from wandering too far for explanations. The metaphorical nature of the meditations kept us on track. Chance alone, the odds against experiencing something relevant to our lives, discounts esoteric explanations such as reliving a past life or observing past, present or future events through some magic looking glass. The relevance of the metaphor to our lives was an undeniable attribute of what we experienced.

Eventually, having identified a similarity between meditations and dreams, we recognized that the source must be our subconscious. Subsequent research confirmed our theory and approximately two years after the first meditation we stumbled across C. G. Jung. There, deep in the cellar of the 'The Portable Jung', we found similar sounding language describing what he called 'Active Imagination'. By this time we had named our process SubContact, ignorant of the protocols that disallow a Jungian from uttering the word 'subconscious'. Frankly, at this point in time we felt that our process was sufficiently our own that we were above the name-calling anyway. And although the prefix 'sub' can set Jungian teeth on edge, we were not about to rechristen our process as 'uncontact'. We believe that there is a difference between the two, and that subconscious is more readily available than is the unconscious. The latter suggests a total lack of awareness.

Such was the heat of our interest in matters relating to psychology that we resumed our formal education. At the time, Dian was 48 and Bob was 58. We both obtained degrees with majors in Psychology. Dian is currently preparing her Masters thesis on mental imaging. Bob has received confirmation of the research for his Ph.D. dissertation on the subject of the personal inventory as a brief therapy. If these subjects of interest sound familiar to you, it must be because you have read the earlier part of this book!

But still, some may ask, besides obtaining degrees in psychology late in life, what benefits can you demonstrate that you can attribute to SubContact? In other words, So What?

What SubContact has done for us

After considerable research, after assessing how our lives had changed from practicing SubContact, we began to evaluate our findings. It was certain that SubContact had benefited our lives well beyond the realm of mental well being. We began to consider publishing our findings. However, to be of value to anyone else, we concluded that SubContact would have to possess four criteria: it would need to be generalizable to a significant portion of the population and conducive to physical, mental and spiritual well being.

Research Conclusions

Conclusion 1: Generalizability

Over the past 10 years we have worked with a variety of individuals. Most have been able to achieve the meditative state that we call SubContact. Some people, a minority, start out in a tentative way, producing what seem like fragmentary pieces of a storyline. Most participants yield a metaphorical story within three sessions. We anticipate that the tentative nature of the initial sessions is attributable to some form of performance anxiety. Once the majority of our participants become aware that there is nothing they can consciously do to produce SubContact material, they relax and are able to experience normal SubContact sessions. The people with the results least useful to themselves were those with the least experience with the modules of SubContact, although everyone reported events that they saw unfold in their mind's eye. Without exception, the more familiar a person was with the modules of SubContact, the more often the person experienced an unbroken storyline, the clearer the imagery and the greater the quality of the metaphorical content the session contained. This supports the following premises:

1. There is direct positive correlation between the frequency of SubContact sessions and quality of experience. That is to say, the more often people practice SubContact, the richer their experience.

2. There is a high probability that anyone who chooses to experience SubContact is capable of doing so.

3. There is direct positive correlation between knowledge of the SubContact modules and the quality of the SubContact experience. That is to say, the more one knows of the SubContact program, the richer their experience.

4. Of particular interest is the positive correlation between the completion of Module 1 and the quality of the SubContact experience. That is to say, the more one knows of Module 1, the richer their SubContact experience. That is why, throughout this book, we have urged the examination of unidentified fears.

Mediating our enthusiasm for everyone trying the program is the caution we have received from SubContact itself that warns that about 5% of the population should not indulge in any type of self-understanding exercise. This figure is supported by the findings of others. C. G. Jung states the same figure (see The Collected Works). Scott Peck, in his book The Road Less Traveled, also cautions that about 5% of people will not profit from psychotherapy.

We believe that there is a self-selecting feature to SubContact that prevents those who should not engage in the practice from doing so. This would probably be manifested as a disinterest in the subject. In extreme cases there would probably be a strong reluctance to the practice of self-examination in those who should not do so.

Conclusion 2: Physical Balance

We also believed that the benefits of SubContact must extend to the physical realm in order to be complementary to the first one. So what evidence can we offer that SubContact is a powerful tool in achieving physical benefits?

There is something symmetrical about life. For example, if there is disproportion in one aspect of life, a countervailing imbalance will arise. So it was with our research into SubContact. We had our regular work to do and took our leisure watching TV when we weren't exploring SubContact. Our minds and spirits were on the rise, but our physical condition left something to be desired. Not necessarily recognizing this, we began to walk in the evening. Pretty soon we were walking faster, and eventually we were walking and jogging.

What could be more logical than to continue this trend with the goal of running a marathon? At least such was the notion that occurred to Bob in a SubContact session. And if Dian was less than enthusiastic about joining him, her enthusiasm was boundless for coaching him toward such an unlikely goal. The decision was made in early July 1993 and the annual Royal Victoria Marathon was scheduled for that October. Given only 90 days to work with, and given the vintage and questionable condition of the body, would it be possible to shape a training program that would get Bob to the finish line 26 miles and 165 yards later? We certainly knew how to find out and began by cramming, what we call information overloading, on what the experts had to say about training for a marathon. At first the news was dismaying; most experts recommended a training period of one year. Once we decided to ignore this advice, we were well on our way. Charts and maps were produced and a training program begun. Somewhere along the way it would be necessary to run 5 miles in order to run 26. And somewhere along the way the 10 and 15-mile barriers must be crossed or there was little point in the undertaking. Mental imaging became a prime tool. In SubContact sessions, a British military character introduced himself. This was an inner mentor, a wise chieftain with unlimited resources who would guide Bob on his quest.

In the event, all did not go exactly according to plan. Oh, Bob completed the course, he even did it jogging the entire distance. However there was a matter of 4 minutes and 54 seconds he would have to answer for; it took him that much longer than the targeted time. Otherwise, the three-month odyssey of training paid off. Bob's mentor, the inner representation, was the only one who harrumphed a bit at missing the final time goal by some 300 seconds.

Let's back up for a moment and take another look at the tools employed to achieve this goal. Some readers may blink once or twice at the mention of a 'military character ... with unlimited resources ... introduced himself'. If that description gave you reason to pause, then we have some great news for you. Each of us has within ourselves the capacity to accomplish almost anything. Bob, for example, had done very little in the area of athletics during his adult life further than to hoist a set of clubs onto the back of a golf cart. Yet through the resources of SubContact, including the creation of a symbolic character of exaggerated courage, the details of preparing for this task were rendered more or less routine.

We urge you to employ such characters in your own SubContact adventures for achieving difficult goals. As we've said elsewhere in this book, if the characters don't already exist, *invent them!* Create them *just as you wish them to be.* One cautionary note: once we create a character, if one hasn't presented themselves first, we are not expected to guide what they say or do. That would contradict the purpose of SubContact.

Having reported Bob's odyssey, we do not rest our physical endurance qualifications on the basis of one of us running a marathon. The fact is that the resources we found in SubContact enabled Dian, for example, to attend classes, write exams and papers and work full time at a demanding job. She did those things and was still in good enough condition to run an equivalent distance to half marathon - which means jogging continuously for two and a half hours.

She graduated with distinction and has completed the coursework for her Masters degree. It is appropriate to mention at this point that Dian had been living with what now appears to be Chronic Fatigue Syndrome for most of her adult life and at the time we lived in Australia was diagnosed with Polymyalgia Rheumatica. Yet somehow, or more specifically through the work she did in SubContact sessions, she uncovered what she believed to be the emotional root cause of her physical ailments. The effect was transforming, giving her personal freedom that enabled her to do things she once thought were impossible for her. Today, she continues to meet the challenges of creating and managing changes in her life.

Bob has since run a second marathon and ran a half marathon in Australia. He did this in spite of having bouts of asthma.

Conclusion 3: Mental Balance

Regarding the next criterion, we would not be writing this book if we had found other than that SubContact is beneficial to mental well being. We hold that physical and mental well being go hand-in-hand. The relationship between mind and body is, to say the least, intimate.

Our experience is that our program is therapeutic. This makes eminent sense when we realize that the objective of SubContact sessions is self-knowledge. It is the aim of almost any psychotherapy to enhance the client's awareness. SubContact is especially powerful in achieving self-knowledge because it delivers messages directly from the individual's subconscious mind. These are notably in the language of a metaphor or parable, which are astonishingly powerful educational methods.

After more than 10 years of studying SubContact sessions, we have concluded that our subconscious minds know what we need to be aware of and when we need to be aware of it. We have never known of anyone being overwhelmed by a message from their subconscious. Like the saying about God, our subconscious will never give us more than we can handle. Often the metaphor or parable contained in a SubContact session will point directly to the new perspective we should consider in order experience spiritual growth.

After years of experience, we have concluded that people who think they are 'channeling' from the lives of other people are in fact experiencing representations from their own subconscious. In other words, any 'people' we meet in

SubContact are aspects of our own personalities and characteristics.

Until a few years ago, Dian's adult life was plagued with recurring bouts of depression. These dark periods often lasted three days and sometimes longer. She endured the classic symptoms such as feelings of anxiety, irritability, pessimism and doubts about her life. At such times, thoughts of death or suicide were not unusual. These cycles of depression could occur at any time and they came to be a part of her adult life.

The bouts of depression stopped after uncovering and examining a series of clues from SubContact. This was not an overnight cure, nor was it drawn out. It seems that there were a series of related incidents in her childhood that had been forgotten. Once brought to the light of day and examined from the perspective of a grown woman, these triggers to depressive cycles disappeared. It required courage, patience and a willingness to engage in self-understanding and the payoff was enormous. Today Dian knows the symptoms of even a small or normal depressive state and has gained the self-knowledge to identify its cause and deal with it.

Although Bob had not been cursed with chronic depression, he did go through a spell of quiet despair when he lost his business in late middle age. Such was the depth of his depression that he plotted his own demise. After a lifetime of relative success Bob found himself broke, unemployed and unemployable. A million-dollar insurance policy, which had been in force for a sufficient time that suicide was covered, stood like a beacon as the direction to take to redeem himself for mistakes that affected his family. As described earlier in Bob's Story, he checked into a hotel room with the intention of ending his life.

Somehow he survived the overdose. In the ensuing year and a half he took himself to AA meetings and struggled to get his life in order. There were mental, physical and spiritual issues to deal with and he was closer in age to the end of his life than the beginning. Without an inkling of what to look for in the search for meaning in his life, without the wit to know it if he saw it, all Bob knew was that God was not finished with him yet. As tales often do, and lives always do, the end of one chapter heralded the beginning of another. One coincidence leads to another until two people find each other and start doing what they were intended to be doing.

Today, Dian and Bob are both notably free of depression. Of course everybody gets down once in a while, but with us a little search for the cause will routinely shine the light on UF or some other hobgoblin lurking in the shadows of our subconscious.

Conclusion 4: Spiritual Quest

This brings us to the final criterion that SubContact had to meet before we would present our findings. As we stated earlier, above all, the practice of SubContact must be spiritual; that is, it must elevate the self-knowledge of the individual, a key element of spiritual growth.

So what do we mean by the phrase spiritual growth? The first thing we mean is that we acknowledge there is a Power greater than ourselves. That Power exists, besides everywhere else, within us. Thus everyone who is on a spiritual quest is, by definition, on a voyage of self-discovery and everyone who is on a voyage of self-discovery is, by definition, on a spiritual quest. Self-knowledge is essential to a spiritual quest. The two are inseparable and each is an aspect of the same polished gem.

> *"To know ourselves, we need to slap the face of fear and wake up our subconscious."*

Nothing New under the Sun

There's nothing new under the sun. Others, much wiser than we, have said more eloquently than we, what we have attempted to say here. The reason we have written this volume is because nobody, to our knowledge, has put it all together between the covers of one book. The importance of what we're saying is that you don't have to take our word for it, but listen to the words that have come to us over the expanse of time. In a way, this is a summary of our book, for we will take the main subject of each of the chapters and tell you what others have said, such as we have been doing throughout this book. We will also provide a bibliography. This is in the spirit of C.G. Jung, who said:

> *"All old truths want a new interpretation, so that they can live on in a new form."*

And as Disraeli said:

> *"The Wisdom of the wise, and the experience of the ages, may be preserved in quotations."*

Quotations By Subject

Change 101 and Fear Quotes

The more I traveled the more I realized that fear makes strangers of people who should be friends - Shirley MacLaine

Everyone believes very easily whatever they fear or desire. - Jean de La Fontaine

It is not death that a man should fear, but he should fear never beginning to live. - Marcus Aelius Aurelius

The meaning I picked, the one that changed my life: Overcome fear, behold wonder. - Æschylus

There are a lot of men who are healthier at age fifty then they have ever been before, because a lot of their fear is gone. - Robert Bly

Some say if only my fears and doubts will leave then I will get to work. But instead you should get to work and then your fears and doubts will leave - Dwight L. Moody

To conquer fear is the beginning of wisdom. - Russell

Do the thing you fear, and the death of fear is certain - Emerson

Courage is not the absence of fear, but rather the judgment that something else is more important than fear - Ambrose Redmoon

In order to change the way we feel we need to change the way we act - Anonymous.

Let us become the change we seek in others - Ghandi

Courage is something you just can't be afraid to have - Anonymous

Power Meditation Quotes

When we pray, we talk to God- when we meditate, we listen - Unknown

If you pray, why worry? If you worry, why pray? - Anonymous.

It is only with the heart that one can see rightly; what is essential is invisible to the eye - Antoine de Saint-Exupery

Ask, and it shall be given you; seek, and ye shall find; knock, and it shall be opened unto you: for every one that asketh receiveth; and he that seeketh findeth; and to him that knocketh it shall be opened - Jesus

Dream Language Quotes

Dreams are illustrations from the book your soul is writing about you - Marsha Norman

When your heart is in your dream, no request is too extreme. -- Jimminy Cricket

4D Thinking Quotes

The significant problems we face cannot be solved at the same level of thinking we were at when we created them - Albert Einstein

Nothing is more powerful than an idea whose time has come - Victor Hugo

The whole of science is nothing more than a refinement of everyday thinking - Albert Einstein

SubContact Quotes

To know yourself you need not to go to any book, to any priest, to any psychologist. The whole treasure is within yourself - Krishnamuti

Do not worry about what others are doing - each of us should turn the searchlight inward and purify his heart as much as possible - Gandhi

I can not know myself until I know God and I can not know God until I know myself - C. S. Lewis

GO Teams Quotes

"When your dreams turn to dust - vacuum!" - Anonymous

"If you haven't got a dream, how you gonna gave a dream come true?" - South Pacific

The End of the Beginning

"Men occasionally stumble over truth, but most of them pick themselves up and hurry off as if nothing had happened." - Winston Churchill

"When one door closes another door opens; but we so often look so long and so regretfully upon the closed door, that we do not see the ones which open for us".
— Alexander Graham Bell

There is a principle which is a bar against all information, which is proof against all arguments and which cannot fail to keep a man in everlasting ignorance – that principle is contempt prior to investigation - Herbert Spencer

"Still ending, and beginning still." - William Cowper

"Every river dreams of the sea."
- Robert K. Benson

Afternote

The WTC attack burned into our psyche that we live in momentous times. September 11 will be as much a turning point in the way people think as was the birth of Christ, the signing of the Magna Carta, the Columbus journey or Pearl Harbor. Yet we are essentially unaware as our minds are reshaped by the tragedy.

Our outer world can change faster than our inner world can accommodate. Our conscious minds reel from seeing jetliners wipe out 6,000 lives and enormous skyscrapers. Beneath the surface, our subconscious minds scrabble to redraw a new world map revised by our vulnerability to evil attack.

Meditation will bring some of the unprocessed material to awareness and enable us to consciously adapt to fears in the most ecological way for the individual. This is true of day-to-day events as well as historical ones. Guided mental imagery, and especially SubContact, can bring to awareness that which needs to be consciously understood and accommodated, thus enabling us to restore mental balance more quickly.

Bibliography

Alcoholics Anonymous (1976, 3rd ed.) Alcoholics Anonymous. New York. Alcoholics Anonymous World Services, Inc.

Bandler, Richard and John Grinder (1979). Frogs into princes. Moab, Montana, Real People Press.

Bradshaw, John (1990). Homecoming: Reclaiming and championing your inner child. New York, Bantam Books.

Campbell, Joseph (1976). The Portable Jung. New York, Penguin Books.

_ (1972). Myths to live by. New York, Viking Press.

Chodorow, Joan (ed., 1997). Jung on active imagination. Princeton, Princeton University Press.

de Bono, Edward (1992). Serious creativity: Using the power of lateral thinking to create new ideas. Toronto, HarperCollins.

- (1972). PO: Beyond yes and no. New York, Pelican Books.

Dilts, Robert (1990). Beliefs. Portland, OR, Metamorphous Press.

Grof, Stanislav (1988). The Adventure of self-discovery. New York, State University of New York Press.

Hay, Louise (1987). You can heal your life. Carlsbad, CA, Hay House.

Joy, W. Brugh (1992). Avalanche. New York, Ballantine Books.

Jung, C. G. (1968). Man and his symbols. New York, Dell Books.

- (1961). Memories, dreams, reflections. New York, Random House - Vintage Books.

Lazarus, Arnold (1977). In the mind's eye. New York, Guilford Press.

Maltz, Maxwell (1969). Psycho-Cybernetics. New York, Pocket Books.

Murphy, Joseph. (1963). The Power of your subconscious mind. Englewood Cliffs, NJ, Prentice-Hall.

Peck, M. Scott (1978). The Road less traveled: A new psychology of love, traditional values and spiritual growth. New York, Simon & Schuster.

Sher, Barbara (1989) Teamworks. New York, WarnerCommunications.

- (1983) Wishcraft: How to get what the you really want. New York, Random House.

VanGundy, Arthur B. (1983). 108 Ways to get a bright idea and increase your creative potential. Englewood Cliffs, NJ, Prentice-Hall.

von Oech, Roger (1988). A Whack on the side of the head. New York, Warner Books.

ISBN 1553690125